ELMIRA

CHILD OF THE STARS

Book 3 of the Issa Trilogy

Kiara Windrider

ISBN

Hardcase 979-8-89322-914-1
Paperback 979-8-89277-996-8

Cover Design:
Katja Cloud © Cloud 7 Design
www.cloud-7-design.de
using AI and Creative Commons Image Pixabay/nicman

Elmira, Child of the Stars, is not a book to be taken lightly. Building upon the first two books of Kiara Windrider's *Issa* trilogy, which offer deep philosophical ideas embedded within personal stories, this volume takes us further on a cosmic journey, into a place of multi-dimensional presence focused within the illusion of time and space.

The insights and predictions within this book, as well as specific information about the coming shift, offer deep understandings about our journey ahead. Shining light at the end of a dark tunnel, Elmira provides us with optimism and hope as we prepare for a quantum leap into an entirely new level of planetary consciousness.

Along with exciting stories continued from the previous books, and including Elmira's own story of how she was chosen to birth a new consciousness, this volume takes us deeper, suggesting that each of us reading this book are an important part of an unfolding story, as we collectively transition to the next stage of human consciousness and the birthing of a new species.

– Francesca Pinoni, therapist and healer, Cyprus

Elmira: Child of the Stars is a captivating book, weaving sacred dimensions, grids, timelines and so much more. The transmission of energy is remarkable, full of eternal loving presence. Kiara has dedicated his life to deepening in the infinite consciousness of love and being of service. This is fully reflected in Elmira's story where we get to be taken on a journey and shown the way love traverses through all things, including the most devastating circumstances, prevailing with planetary love and vitality that is eternal. This is for all those on an evolutionary journey, who seek to understand and participate in these exciting times of shift!

– Laura Sontrop, therapist and coach, Canada

Tears are running down my face as I read these words of deep remembrance. I am spellbound. The truth, the wisdom, and the light of the words are impeccable. Elmira's message creates an entirely different pathway for earth and humankind. It is a deep joy to read and feel what you write, and what you are reminding us of.

– Jonette Crowley, author of *The Eagle and the Condor*, USA

Table of Contents

Prologue..9

Part I
Soul of the Earth

Chapter 1   Magic..13

Chapter 2   Memories 15

Chapter 3   Aisha..18

Chapter 4   The Great Plan...22

Chapter 5   Puddles of Time 24

Chapter 6   The Great Activation..27

Chapter 7   Adventures with the Fae 31

Chapter 8   Tuatha de Danann..34

Chapter 9   Hiranya and Arwyn...37

Chapter 10   Eliyakim and Sara...40

Chapter 11   Inner Earth...44

Chapter 12   The Seventh Initiation 47

Chapter 13   Dreams...49

Chapter 14   Timelines 51

Chapter 15   Soul of the Earth 54

Chapter 16   Stagnation 57

Chapter 17   Dragon Riders 59

Chapter 18   Akashic Records 61

Chapter 19   Morphogenetic Fields 63

Chapter 20   Planetary Hierarchies 65

Chapter 21   Four Faces of the Mother 67

Chapter 22   Quantum Shift 69

Chapter 23   Dwapara Yuga 71

Chapter 24   Guild of Merlins..74

Chapter 25   Physicality 77

Chapter 26   Magnetic Fields 80

Chapter 27   Scourge of Christianity 82

Chapter 28   The Grail Kings 85

Chapter 29   The Saturnian Matrix......................................88

Chapter 30   Christ Consciousness Grid 91

Chapter 31   Alchemy 93

Chapter 32   Gaia 95

Chapter 33   Earth Goddess..98

Chapter 34   Collective Fields 101

Chapter 35   Light of Hope 103

Chapter 36   Time Bubbles 105

Chapter 37   Mind of Light 108

Chapter 38   Body of Light...111

Part II
Soul of the Universe

Chapter 39   Transitions 115

Chapter 40   Multi-Dimensionality.................................117

Chapter 41   Evolutionary Plan.......................................120

Chapter 42   Plasma Cosmology 123

Chapter 43   Cosmic Seeding...126

Chapter 44   Shambala..128

Chapter 45   Choice Point 131

Chapter 46   Underworld Journey....................................134

Chapter 47   The Choice 137

Chapter 48   The Whales...140

Chapter 49   Mirra Alfassa 144

Chapter 50   The Meeting 147

Chapter 51   Supramental Descent....................................150

Chapter 52   Supramental Catastrophe 153

Chapter 53   The Journey Ahead 156

Chapter 54   Cycle of the Yugas 159

Chapter 55   Galactic Superwave 162

Chapter 56   Heliopause Breakthrough 165

Chapter 57   Cosmic Ray Bombardment 168

Chapter 58   Solar Events..171

Chapter 59   Magnetic Reversal 174

Chapter 60   DMT Release..177

Chapter 61   Crustal Plate Displacement 180

Chapter 62   Dimensional Shift 183

Chapter 63   Second Sun 186

Chapter 64   Supramental Transformation 190

Chapter 65   The Inconscient 194

Chapter 66   Seventh Universe..197

Chapter 67   Gaia Luminous..200

Chapter 68   Himalayan Outpost.......................................203

Chapter 69   The Supramental World..................................206

Chapter 70   Children of the Stars 209

Epilogue..213

Glossary 215

About Kiara Windrider..219

Prologue

What you hold in your hands is the third manuscript in the Issa trilogy, the book that my ancestor Jerael had long sought but failed to find. It has remained hidden across the span of time until a time when the events revealed within are due to take place.

Jerael is revered in the Gnostic communities as one who discovered two manuscripts, *Issa Son of the Sun,* and *Mirjan Daughter of the Moon*, which were both written hundreds of years ago in the beginning of the Christian era. They were circulated within the Gnostic communities in what is now known as France.

Before he died, Jerael made mention of a third manuscript that was written later, and completes the story. If you have opened this book, it is because you yourself are part of this story.

Where this manuscript was hidden in order to be discovered in due time is another tale. Jerael had left some clues, and it was up to me, many generations later, to follow these up. Discovering the manuscript was an initiation in itself, for I had to enter a crack in the fabric of time in order to do so, guided by the presence of Elmira herself.

I was given the task of translating this ancient manuscript for a modern age. This has taken a lifetime of preparation. As I finish translating this manuscript, a passage from another ancient scripture comes to mind, inspired undoubtedly by the same mystic forces that shaped the story within these pages:

"Possible it is to lead meekly the wild rutting tuskers, breaking the stakes they are tied with. Possible it is to befriend the bear and speak with wolves. Possible it is to ride peacefully on the lion's back. Possible it is to inhabit and dance with a snake. Possible it is to turn to gold the five metals by melting them in fire, suffusing them with mercury, and catalyzing them with a mystic compound.

Possible it is to move about this earth unseen by any person, and even walk beneath the earth. Possible it is to meet the heavenly beings. Possible it is to stay young everlastingly. Possible it is to pass into other's bodies or change the shape of your own. Possible it is to walk on the waters and to stop your own breath. Possible it is to sit unscathed amidst the tongues of fire. Possible it is to command marvelous powers beyond one's reach. But oh heavens, how hard it is to control my own mind, and to keep it in stillness."

— Sacred Hymns of Thayumanavar

PART I

SOUL OF THE EARTH

Chapter 1

Magic

It all started with the elder dragons. Across filaments of time and space they wove together the fabric of the universe. Wormholes were built and dimensions were created. And then from the breath of the dragons, worlds came into being teeming with senses and life.

The elder dragons rest between cycles of time, dreaming new worlds into existence. At the dawning of a universal age they begin to stir and awaken. They seek for those who are born to ride them, who then take incarnation on worlds chosen to initiate a new cycle.

My brother Hiranya is one of these dragon riders, fused with the power of the elder dragons. I will say more about him in the pages that follow, and of those that could cross through dimensions and tame the fires of creation.

My brother Eliyakim was one who had learned to tame these fires, and formed a lineage of *starwalkers,* whose destiny was to prepare the earth for the forces that were to move through her planetary body.

And I, Elmira, am an invisible seed, awakening within the tree of life known as *ashwatta,* which has roots above sourced in the center of all things, and branches below intertwining through hundreds of created worlds and dimensions, to birth a species that could ride with the dragons, across the vastness of creation, even out beyond the fabric of time and space itself.

People know me today as the daughter of Issa and Mirjan (pronounced Mir-aan), rulers of the land of Kash. I also became known to the world as Child of the Stars, for this is the destiny woven for me by those who brought me to this Earth, and invited me to join with them in initiating a new race of humanity. But I do not like long names or titles, and you can simply call me Mira.

If you are discovering this story for the first time, you may be feeling a bit confused by all the similar sounding names. There is my mother Mirjan and my grandmother Maryam, who was mother of Issa. There is Issa's first love, Mari, and then there is me, Mira. As you will learn later, there is another in our soul family, born very close to your own time, who also plays an important role in the great awakening. But *mer* is also the sea, the *mother of all things,* reflecting the universal ocean, which connects all things together.

The first two books in this trilogy of life, *Son of the Sun* and *Daughter of the Moon* were scripted by my mother, Mirjan, and describe the grand journey of awakening which my parents undertook with the help of their many teachers. My beloved mother had a gift for writing, her heart, mind and spirit fused with the voice of the *Great Mother,* joining together to weave a story that inevitably touched the soul.

Before she ascended, along with Issa, to her next sphere of service, my mother wished that I complete the story that she began, and share it with the world. I will attempt, in my own quiet way, to continue where she left off, for *Child of the Stars* moves through many generations, many timelines, and many dimensions of existence.

Like a river flowing back to the sea, this story has no beginning or end, but for those who might be curious, I am delighted to share a next chapter in the great tapestry of this unfolding journey.

Chapter 2

Memories

My story begins with my memories, and my memories extend back to a time before I ever took birth in this current body.

I grew up listening to the currents of sound sparkling through the center of all things, the sap that moved inside the living bark of a tree, the rhythmic beat of a hummingbird's wings, the voice of an eagle calling to its mate, the rainbow trout shimmering through icy glacier streams.

From the time I was very young, my beloved parents understood I was here on this earth as an ambassador from the stars, and taught me what I needed to keep the doorway open to worlds beyond the physical. The currents of life moved through my body as a sparkling river of joy, which I was taught to navigate like a seaman sailing across deep oceans following the fixed rhythms of a starry night.

We were perhaps an unusual family. I don't remember a time when we were not touched by the voice of the *Great Mother*. My own beautiful mother lived only to serve Her, as did her extraordinary teacher Aisha, who later became my own precious teacher as well.

And what can I say about my beloved father Issa, who had travelled the world and then returned to his own doorstep to find that most precious of life's gifts, the love of a woman who knew how to fuse her body with the earth and her spirit to the skies!

I do not know how it was with other children my age, but my parents entrusted me to the *Earth Mother* from the moment I touched this earth, recognizing that I was here by her invitation, and that I would be kept safe in her playground of life.

And so it was, that before I could even walk, I had learned to swim, and was at home in the frigid waters of the glacial mountain lakes where the water fairies would teach me about portals existing within my own body, in the space between cells, which crossed over to dimensions outside of the physical worlds, where the river of time moved differently, and where I could join my spirit to the spirit that moved through all things.

I was very young when my grandmother died. She had followed the path of her destiny across an entire continent so she could give birth to my father in the land of our ancestors in the west, returning eventually to the paradise valley in Kashmir which became our home. Her name was Maryam, which means pure, or graced with devotion, as she indeed was.

She had left for Gandhara to visit our grand uncle Yosef, also known as Gondophorus. She came to me in my dreams one night and told me that she was following the river of stars back to her other home, and that she would meet me there. She told me not to cry for her because she would never be gone from my life and my vision.

And so it was. When news came of her passing and my parents grieved, I continued to see her and speak with her as she moved through the passage between worlds. She came to me in my dreams, and then she would speak with me in my waking story wherever I was and whenever I wished. She would speak to me of the worlds she travelled through, which mirrored the worlds of physical form, which shaped and formed them. I would speak these messages to my beloved father, for he had loved her dearly and missed her physical presence.

It was the water spirits who taught me to enter these worlds, and to walk through a river across the stars. As I entered this river, I would find myself stretched across the sky, and my body would draw breath from the substance of this river of light. I discovered I could stay under the frigid waters of our mountain lake longer than my brothers could, or even my parents.

It was only later that I discovered this ability to hold breath was considered unusual. The water spirits were my first teachers. They told me once that they had looked for my spirit across the vast river of time because the *Great Mother* had need of me, that I had been woven together fresh from starlight to join with the heart of *Earth Mother* on her path of rebirth.

All these things I knew, although I couldn't say how, for this is how it had always been through all my memories of time.

There was also my grandmother on my mother's side. Zuhaira was her name, which means *North Star* in our language, as indeed she was in my own mother's life, and for all those who knew her.

It was she who told me, when I was old enough to understand, that she had dreamed of me before I arrived, and heard my name being given to me by the spirit elders. *El* refers to the heavens, the great skies above, and *Mira* means woman, so my name means *sky woman,* or *child of the stars.* She it was who had given this secret name to my mother when it became time to invite me down to this earth.

I could not have been blessed with a more beautiful family.

Chapter 3

Aisha

And then of course there is my beloved teacher Aisha, who was also teacher for my beautiful mother. Every time I think of her, I feel her as great filaments of cosmic starlight moving through each cell of my human body. She is never far from me, for she has become in some mysterious way the soul of the *Earth Mother*, although she still shows up in my vision as when I first knew her.

Aisha encouraged me to remember what I already knew, even when I did not know that I knew. She could see through the illusion of the *kanchukas*, the five aspects of a veil known as *maya*, and helped me travel the rainbow path up to the blue star heart of the *Great Mother*. She helped me trust my path of destiny when everything seemed too big to contain in one tiny human form.

I remember well the time when Aisha took our family deep into the bowels of the earth, where we encountered the *Guardians*. I was still a young child then, but old enough to feel the tremendous excitement in my spirit when she asked if I would be willing to become a biological representative for the next root race.

Of course I said yes, for this was the very purpose of my existence, and aligned with the wishes of the *Great Mother*. Contrary to the assumptions of many, our current root race is but a transitional species, destined to exist only within the current cycle of Ages. Its role within the vast tapestry of evolutionary cycles has been to cultivate a functional ego, a sense of unique identity within the interconnected unity of all things. Yet, this is merely an intermediary stage.

There are many species of life found across infinite star systems. Some races exhibit profound intelligence and spiritual advancement, while others are driven only by conquest and destruction. Many worlds and lifeforms have been destroyed in mindless galactic wars.

This echoes what you have experienced in the history of your own planet. Within the enormous potential for goodness and diversity, a genetic flaw inherent in the very structure of duality has stunted the evolution of the soul, allowing aggression, dominance and greed to distort and overcome the delicate balance of life.

So at the very beginning of the current cycle of *yugas*, symbolically intertwined with the story of Eve and the apple, a decision was made in the evolutionary councils to evolve a species that was capable of remembering its connection with creator source, while at the same time fully embodying the diversity of creation, a species destined to shine through galaxies of stars as a perfected template of divine manifestation.

The *tree of knowledge* would be harmonized with the *tree of life*, symbolizing the ability to touch both earth and sky. It signified the ability to embody unified consciousness while remaining anchored within the physical form, enabling a flow of creative power directly from the heart of the *Great Mother*, unhindered by the veiling power of the *kanchukas*.

However, unrestricted creativity is a dangerous gift. Imagine a child being told they can have anything they want at any given moment. A child has not learned yet the maturity of wisdom that comes with experience, and is capable of making mistakes that lead to the accumulation of pain.

Similarly, as a species in transition, you have learned to think but not yet to understand, to act but not yet to grasp the vast consequences of each action.

And therefore, there needed to be a transitional state between tasting from the tree of knowledge and embodying the tree of life.

Having tasted of the tree of knowledge, humans have aspired to godlike status, playing with choices offered by a mind that has become increasingly capable of thought and reason. However, without understanding the laws of reciprocity and the balance of life, a personal ego, or *ahamkara*, has emerged, which has been pitted against the needs and demands of a greater wholeness.

It is a dangerous gift, for it means the *Great Mother* has placed the power of creation, but also vast destruction, into the hands of a race still in infancy. Can you learn about maturity and wisdom as you cross the threshold of a new age, or will you destroy your earthly home in the fires of infantile arrogance, as has tragically happened so many times in galactic history?

The Guardians tell us that in the fulness of time, a new species is destined to emerge from the underworld of the current species, a Sixth Root Race, or *homo luminous*. It will be biologically and vibrationally different, providing access to the tree of life inherent in the heart of each human. A Seventh Root Race will shortly follow, which Aisha calls *homo universalis*, a *gnostic* species with the capacity to contain the power of the dragons and to create entire universes.

The universe is a single organism. As these new species come into form, their vibrational resonance will affect the entire spectrum of life across all the galaxies of creation. A wave of unity consciousness will ripple across all worlds and dimensions, awakening the seed of light within all creatures great and small. Galactic wars will cease. Balance will be restored. Eons of suffering and darkness will come to an end as a seventh universe comes into being.

Dear ones, you have penetrated the heart of darkness. Now it is time to embody the fullness of light. This is your collective journey as you transition from duality into unity. In some way that I cannot fully explain, the matrix for these new races was woven into my subtle bodies before I took birth on this earth. I am to help birth the luminous potential of a sun-eyed species as humanity grows beyond infancy towards maturity.

Chapter 4

The Great Plan

You must forgive me, for there are times when I find myself entering the heart of Aisha, in her current embodiment as soul of this Earth. And when this happens, I find myself speaking from this place above and beyond the personal self which looks out through the eyes of Elmira. My words change, and the energy moving through my body no longer belongs to a human self, no longer fixed in a single stream of time.

I do not wish to be other than what you see before you, a most ordinary woman born of earth and married to the earth. But at the same time, I am a child of the stars, tasked with the destiny of reflecting what humanity will one day grow into, and which is becoming increasingly manifest within me. Aisha tells me that those who are drawn to this manuscript will themselves share this destiny, that she will work with them as she continues to work with me, to embody new codes of starlight within these precious human bodies.

Embodiment is not an easy task. Those who are reading this in a time still to come will be warrior souls invited to earth from across the stars to support her evolutionary journey during the turning of an age. You will feel you do not belong here, and wish to go back to other homes. You will feel that this task is too great, that you will never be enough, that it is much too difficult to remember after being lost so long in the density of matter.

Some of you will recognize that the journey of awakening is not a personal journey but a collective event. You will find yourself disheartened by how far your human species has separated itself from the circle of life, and wrought so much destruction upon this earth. You might even wonder if you are close to an extinction event, and whether humans deserve to survive into another age.

I feel these things, for I have journeyed deep into your collective psyche, including the vast history of fragmentation and pain. My identity is no longer held within a single stream of time. I feel the unveiling of future possibilities passing through my consciousness, and it sometimes frightens me. Were it not for Aisha's presence within me I would feel immensely lost as I walk through these strands of time, for I see how far your race has tipped towards self-centeredness and spiritual isolation, how close you have come to destroying yourselves and the extended circle of life.

And yet I speak to you of hope. Do not be afraid. A dark night still lies ahead, but it is a night where all that is hidden will be revealed, where everything that is lost will find its way back to the heart of the *Great Mother*. In the right time, and if you so wish, I will speak more of this journey that lies ahead, for you are still a precious jewel in the eyes of the *Mother*, with a destiny and purpose far greater than you have ever imagined.

It is important you know this so you do not lose yourself in feelings of impotence, fear and despair, and so you can prepare yourself for the great task that lies ahead.

Chapter 5

Puddles of Time

And now let me return to my own time, and take up events from where my mother left off. As I have said, she had a gift for writing, and could describe events beautifully as experienced by a single arrow of time. In contrast, I find myself jumping from one timeline to another in the writing of this story, for this is how I experience myself.

I hope this does not become tiresome for those of you accustomed to a more linear mode of story-telling. But it has the advantage of allowing me to fit more pieces of the puzzle together, and relate more directly to your own time. For although I have aged only a few hundred years at the time of this writing, I can look across time and meet you wherever you are, even into the 21st century where I perceive many of you reading this have presently taken birth.

I can meet you in these pages, those of you who are still reading this manuscript, and I can meet you also within your dreams and your own questioning heart. For as I have said, I represent the template of a new humanity coming into being, awakening within each of you as your perfected divine self.

With that said, I will update you from within my own time. My beloved mother ended her manuscript with the return of Issa into France and

Britain, as these lands later became known. He had travelled there with my brothers Hiranya and Eliyakim, and experienced a chance meeting with Sara, his daughter through Mari of Magadha, who became known in later times as Mary Magdalene.

The four of them had been guided west and north towards a mysterious island that sometimes appeared in the mists known as Avalon. Known as a temple of initiation for female priestesses, the leader of the priestess clan had seen fit to invite the three men as well as Sara to her sacred isle, for the time had come when men and women were to come together in sacred ceremony to unveil the mysteries of the coming age.

Many were the teachings and gifts exchanged here, but when it was time for Issa to continue his journey with the boys, Sara realized she was being called to remain in Avalon a while longer, and to complete her own training as a priestess. It was a difficult choice, for the time she had spent with her father and half-brothers was precious to her. But she also realized she could not ignore this higher calling, and that she would see her family again.

Issa held his daughter close as they said goodbye, for he had been deeply touched by her presence, and immensely grateful for the time they had been given together. Eliyakim and Sara too had created a special bond with each other, and knew that their time together was not yet done.

If this was Mirjan's story, she might have spoken further of the many adventures the three men experienced along the way as they made their way north through wild country and warring tribes. Forgive me, I am not as good a story teller as my mother was. From my own perspective in time, I tend to focus on the bigger story rather than specific events, and might therefore move through an entire sequence of events far more rapidly than those events deserve.

But as they made their way through wild country, the three of them were warmly welcomed by tribal chieftains everywhere they travelled, first in Wales and later in Ireland, where the boys were initiated into the mysteries of the Earth, and came to fulfil their own destinies in the circle of life. I will speak more of this in the course of time, for my brothers and

I have always been inseparably linked, even when separated by distance and time.

Issa never did find Mari of Magadha. She had travelled on to the region of Ephesus within the Eastern Roman Empire, where she had now settled, along with John the Beloved, and others within the early community of disciples. She was much revered here as a teacher, and brought great comfort to the hearts of many. She died at a ripe old age in the grottos above the city of Ephesus. Her last home is still recognized in your present-day Turkey as *House of the Mother*, or *Meryemana Ev*.

Chapter 6

The Great Activation

There is a grand design to everything, including the writing of this manuscript. I started with the idea that I was writing a story, but very quickly realized that it was more about preparing the hearts of those who were themselves part of the story, speaking to the challenges they would face, and the gifts that would unfold on this journey of embodiment.

To those of you reading this, the pathway to the new species is not a linear process. Although it may have taken a thousand years to prepare the ground, and another thousand years to achieve the first signs of activation, the rest of the work could happen very quickly.

When the time is right, when the magnetic fields are aligned, a new root race can be birthed in the space of a heartbeat, a moment in time when the five *koshas* disengage from each other, releasing the weight of subconscious history, then re-aligning with the blueprint of a sixth root race which I am learning to create in collaboration with Aisha.

Aisha calls this the *Great Activation*. For some, especially for the first pioneers, this will happen in stages, requiring multiple journeys into the underworld to transmute encrusted layers of collective trauma. This process is sometimes known as the *dark night of the soul*. This is not an easy task, and many will wish to give up. For others, if they are empty enough, and if they understand the way, it could happen in a brief moment of time, as primordial light penetrates into dense layers of mind and body.

Eventually, there will come a collective activation, a global manifestation of primordial light, and the new species will be birthed. I will speak to this in more detail later in this manuscript, for it is the main purpose of my being.

Aisha first made the journey into the underworld with Issa after he was crucified on a Roman cross, along with Mirjan and Chetan Nath. Their collective intention opened a door within the collective psyche of your current root race. Deep layers of density were released, although much remains still that must also be brought to the surface.

Aisha entered deeply enough into the underworld that she was enabled to transmute her physical body into a body of light, then merge her soul with the soul of the Earth. This was not an easy task, and without all the years of preparation, and without the presence of Mirjan to guide her back, she might not have succeeded, and could even have found herself imprisoned in that density, as many indeed have.

The journey into the underworld is equivalent to the opening of Pandora's box, as hinted within that ancient Greek myth. The box was never meant to be kept closed forever, for the human species is designed to question everything, and jump headlong into the great unknown. But it was opened too quickly without proper guidance and preparation, and the result was an overwhelming profusion of new potentials.

The ills released into the world in that moment came not from the box itself, but from Pandora's inability to integrate those potentials. The same forces that grant power to the gods can also, when not properly understood or channeled, create violent catastrophes.

This is what took place at the Fall of Man, as described symbolically in the Sumerian scriptures. Knowledge without discernment, and power without embodiment, is dangerous. It has led to long millennia of dualistic thought, where reason and argument became the only measure of truth.

The dark ages of humanity which preceded the scientific revolution reflect the brutality that humans are capable of when disconnected from the tree of life.

The dark ages are not over, as you have yourselves experienced in the wars and manipulations of the 20th and early 21st centuries. Within the cycles of time, however, the *kali yuga* has given way to the *dwapara yuga*, a transitional age when all things are being questioned, and new pathways are being opened. In the rotational cycle of your Sun around its twin star, Sirius, you are moving closer now to the Galactic Source, allowing the light of the *Galactic Mother* to initiate a new cycle of human and planetary evolution.

This is where you stand now. I chuckle to think that your reckoning of linear time has become somehow linked with the advent of my own father. Be that as it may be, you are nearing the end of an age dominated by linear time. As you shift towards an *age of light*, reflected first within the *treta yuga*, and then the *satya yuga*, your experience of time itself will change.

Time will no longer remain a straight arrow of history moving from a nebulous past to an unknown future. You will find, as I have been experiencing already, that events are linked together not within time but through vibrational resonance. You attract people and circumstances into your life based on this resonance. You experience worlds and dimensions mirroring your vibrational resonance.

And when the moment arrives, a new age of planetary history will begin in much the same way. You are galactic seeds birthed on this Earth to initiate a return journey. This cannot be measured in linear time. Even one of you awakening fully within cellular form is enough to catalyze the activation of an entirely new species.

The Sixth Sun of the Incas, the Fifth World of the Hopi, the Satya Yuga of the Vedic seers — these prophecies do not reflect a linear progression of ages. Rather, they refer to what your modern physicists call a quantum leap in consciousness. This is what you prepare for now, and this is what I am here to support you with, as is Aisha and the *Great Mother* herself.

Meanwhile, have you wondered how a woman whose physical consciousness rests in a human form hundreds of years in your past is aware of things that you are just now learning and discovering? As I have said, my consciousness is not locked in a linear mode of time, and I have travelled much further even than your own time, beyond the *Great Activation*, and into source dimensions beyond your current third dimensional world.

It is thus that I can share with you about this journey, and offer you a message of certainty and hope, the same Hope that remained lost at the bottom of Pandora's box until it was ready to be opened once again.

Chapter 7

Adventures with the Fae

Let us go back now to my elder brother Hiranya, for that story is still incomplete.

There was always something special about him, and his relationship with the worlds of nature. This became enhanced when Aisha took us into the inner caverns of the earth, where Aranyani, the elusive goddess of wilderness came to him from among the *Guardians of the Earth,* and chose him as her student.

Aranyani represents the untouched beauty of the forest, and embodies the wild, untamed aspects of nature. She symbolizes the harmony and balance found in the natural world, and is also the patron for tribes of humans who remained in higher dimensional form at the end of the Lemurian cycle when the majority of humans fell into third density.

The *apsaras* and *gandharvas, yakshas, kinnaras,* and *nagas* represent some of these tribes. Aranyani had introduced Hiranya to many of them, and showed him how he could move between the worlds and communicate with them just as easily as with humans in third density. They would simply step down their vibrational frequency even as he raised up his own, and they would meet in the middle.

And so he was never alone in the forest, where he would disappear for days or weeks at a time in his younger days. Sometimes beings from the inner earth would invite him to visit their homes in etheric dimensions beneath the earth, and he learned to shift between dimensions as easily as any of them.

He was never in danger in the forests, for under the protection of Aranyani, these nature tribes would offer him food when he found nothing to eat, and provide an aura of radiance where even fierce predators would instantly befriend him.

And so, as Issa and his sons left Avalon, and travelled through the forests of Wales and Ireland, these same forest tribes stood guard over them wherever they went. They were known here as the *fae* people, or the *elfen* tribes, and included the *tylwyth teg,* the *sidhe* and the *tuatha de danann*.

People in your time seem to think of these beings as mythological creatures, just like unicorns, yeti and dragons, but it is not so. Just because your own subtle senses have deteriorated to a point where you can no longer travel or perceive across dimensions, it does not mean that these forest dwellers are any less real than your own tribes and communities.

Although Hiranya had a special gift bestowed to him by Aranyani, all three of them were able to look beyond the physical dimensions and interact with these magical beings, who had chosen to remain in a state of primordial oneness with the natural worlds. For Issa, who had spent so much of his life exploring and questioning the spiritual traditions of the world, it was a welcome change to simply open to the natural flow of life in these primal forests, just as he had experienced in his own boyhood with Sara's mother in Magadha.

And just as Mirjan had learned to merge her consciousness with his while he was away in Palestine, and follow him in his journeys, so Issa had now learned to do the same with Mirjan. It had become increasingly clear to both of them that the boys were ready to follow their own paths of destiny, and that it was time now for the two of them to continue their own shared mission, including the path of the rainbow body. And of course Issa missed me, Elmira, as well, just as I often missed just snuggling up to his physical presence. It was time to go home, he decided.

Issa's decision to return to Kashmir was an emotional moment for him as well as the boys, for neither of them knew whether or when they would see each other again. But they had forged a bond that went beyond outer veils of communication, and they knew they would remain deeply connected in the inner worlds, and continue to meet and support each other as needed.

The two boys continued their journey after Issa's departure. There was no hurry to get anyplace, and it was a time of deep bonding between the brothers, and also with the forest creatures. Sometimes the elven tribes would ask them to settle disputes among them, or invite them to follow them into dimensions within the earth where time moved differently. They even showed the boys how it was possible to enter portals beneath the earth and emerge through another portal hundreds of miles away.

Years passed, and the two brothers had come to feel very much at home in the forest world. During the winters they would be invited to sheltered glades beneath the earth, where they always came to be accepted as one of the elven people. It was a magical and exhilarating time, filled with feasting, music and joy.

But then one day Eliyakim found himself missing Sara. They had been communing with each other often in the inner worlds. Sara had finished her studies as a priestess of Avalon, and they both realized they had a destiny with each other, and that it was time to fulfil this.

And so the brothers took leave of each other, knowing they would always remain connected through the forest people, and would find each other no matter where they were in this life.

Chapter 8

Tuatha de Danann

As Hiranya continued his travels through the Irish forests, he would often feel the breath of Aranyani guiding him, especially now that he was on his own. One day she told him that he would be meeting someone that he had a destiny with, and that he was to prepare himself.

He had been travelling through the western lands, near a mountain shaped like the head of a dragon. A small spring flowed down from rocks laced with lichen and clover. Hiranya found a crack within the mountain, and decided this would be a good place for a vigil, as he had been taught by his beautiful forest guide.

Drinking only the clear water from the spring, and munching occasionally on leaves of clover, he slowed his breath and heartbeat to become more receptive to subtle dimensions. Suddenly Aranyani showed up to greet her favorite student. Hiranya rapturously rose to embrace her, as she flashed her own smile of playful delight. Hiranya felt her always in his journeys through the forest, but it had been a while since they had seen each other in the physical realm.

Aranyani invited him to follow her into the mountain. Aisha had taught us about projecting our consciousness into rocks and trees, and walking through portals into parallel realms of existence. We had practiced this until it was second nature to us. Now, with Aranyani guiding him, he found himself moving easily past an energetic barrier, and entering into the heart of the mountain.

They found themselves in a passage winding downward, lit by a row of torches leading into a circular chamber carved into the mountain. Hundreds of people were gathered here wearing brightly colored tunics of every hue imaginable. They seemed to be waiting for something.

They bowed their heads in silent greeting as Aranyani walked in, closely followed by Hiranya. The King of the Mountain, recognizable by a circlet of gold around his head, walked up to meet Aranyani.

"Welcome back to our little kingdom, dear sister" he smiled broadly as he embraced her. "You told us you would be coming, and we have waited eagerly for your arrival."

"And who is this young man you have brought with you?" he enquired, as he appraised Hiranya's slim but sturdy physique, long flaxen curls, and gentle green eyes.

"This is he who I have been telling you about," said Aranyani. "His name is Hiranya, which means *stag* in our Kashmiri language, and he is here in answer to prophecy. I have watched over him all his life, and taught him the ways of the forest. He knows and understands the wild creatures, and I find his heart strong and pure as the winter snows."

Hiranya found himself blushing as he listened to Aranyani's words, but held the king's gaze. The king's eyes twinkled as he observed the young man standing before him.

"Welcome to our little mountain kingdom, my son," he spoke at length, gathering Hiranya into a sturdy embrace. "We have heard about you, and awaited you here with great anticipation and rejoicing."

"My name is Nuada. We are the Tuatha de Danann," he went on, "a tribe of elder people who thrived for long centuries on this land before the arrival of Celtic invaders, long before the power of the great dragons was broken."

"We were dragon riders in the old days, harnessing the power of these ancient beings to build and maintain the circle of life. And then came the invaders who used dark magic to corrupt the earth, destroy the woodlands, and sow discord amongst the original people. We went to war with each other, but were eventually defeated at the battle of Talitiu.

"In a final rite of dragon magic, an alternate dimension was created for us, known as the *otherworld*. It is here that Aranyani has brought you. We live in peace within this mountain, and within the forests of this vast region, where we can observe, invisible and unseen, events that transpire in the outer world.

"Our prophecies proclaim the arrival of one who would someday create a bridge between our worlds, and bring peace to this land." He paused, then went on. "Do you understand what I speak, my son?"

Chapter 9

Hiranya and Arwyn

All right, so I was wrong. I too can be a storyteller when I want to be, just like my mother, and I actually find this quite enjoyable. It helps me enter more fully into my human personality and human history, which is quite refreshing from time to time. It is also such a joy to connect again with my beautiful brothers, who will remain within my memories forever. All things are connected, and I will continue the story.

Hiranya felt shaken as he absorbed the impact of Nuada's words. He did not doubt the prophecy, for he had felt these same threads of destiny within himself. But he was loath to imagine that his happy care-free existence might come to an end if he took up the *fae* cause as his own.

And then his gaze swept across the room to meet the shining emerald eyes of a young woman standing in the shadows. With hair like spun gold, her features reflected the luminous beauty of her elfin race, exuding a serenity, grace, and gentle power he had never experienced from anyone in his young life. He was instantly smitten. Gasping for breath, heart lurching in sudden confusion, he strove to maintain his composure as Nuada's eyes softly crinkled in amusement.

"This is my daughter, Arwyn." His voice betrayed the great pride he felt in her. "She has dreamed of your coming many moons ago, even before my sister Aranyani showed up to announce your visit. I see you will have much to talk about."

And so began a new chapter in Hiranya's life. Aranyani smiled fondly as she hugged him goodbye. She had completed her task of match-making, and vanished in a flash of light. Hiranya and Arwyn soon began to spend all their time with each other. It was a wondrous and transformative experience for both. They were of different races, and different vibrational densities, but it didn't seem to matter, for Hiranya had learned to move between dimensions at will, entering an expanded space where his senses could grasp the subtle qualities of either world.

He found his senses awakening to a realm of enchantment and mystery beyond his wildest dreams. Arwyn's ethereal beauty and radiant aura matched his own, and her presence pulled him deep into the world of the *fae*, igniting a fascination for ancient knowledge, and a thirst for understanding the most profound secrets of existence.

Arwyn's world was a realm where magic and divine power came together. Tuatha de Danann were an ancient people who understood the balance of nature, and maintained a relationship with elemental spirits, which races of men had forgotten. Their mythologies held a memory of how it was to be fused with the power of the ancient dragons to create worlds of harmony and beauty.

Their love for each other transcended the boundaries between mortal and *fae*, bridging worlds that were often thought to be separate. Although their divergent realms were sometimes challenging to reconcile, they were willing to learn from each other, and find strength in their bond.

Among the Tuath de Danann, Hiranya became known as the *Green Man*, for he could talk with the trees and make them grow, and walk on forest trails followed by all manner of wild creatures. Among humans, when they ventured out together, he became known as *Pan,* for he could move in and out of dimensions at will, revealing himself to those who were willing to learn of nature and magic.

Although they much preferred to be with the *fae*, Arwyn and Hiranya also began to spend time in the human world, for they realized that this is where they were needed the most. It was not difficult for Arwyn to lower her vibrational frequency and allow herself to be seen by humans, and they would often travel vast distances, repairing the leylines where they had been damaged, and restoring the power of the elemental worlds.

If Hiranya had a special affinity for trees and dryads, Arwyn had an affinity for water and undines. Perhaps this is why I myself felt such a fondness for her, for the water elementals are close to my own heart as well. Subtle melodies of song would follow them as they walked along streams and lakes, for the undines love music, and felt charmed by her presence. In times to come, she became known to them as the *Lady of the Lake.*

With the passage of time, a new challenge presented itself. While among the *fae*, Hiranya discovered that time passed slowly, and many years could pass with no outward signs of aging. But in the outside world, he found himself aging quickly. His long curly locks began to show signs of grey, and eventually turned white.

Arwyn could have remained youthful for long years had she remained in the timeless realms of the Tuath de Danann. But with all the time she was spending in human habitation, fulfilling their task of creating a bridge between the two races, she too began to show signs of aging. Nevertheless, their task was to establish an order of Elder Druids, a mystery school for humans who wished to learn of the *fae*, and understand the magic and mysteries of nature.

Hiranya was acknowledged as leader of these Druids, the first of an order of Merlins. Just like the falcon Horus in ancient Egypt, Merlins became known as messengers and seers who had learned to cross between the worlds, in order to offer wisdom and guidance for those in need.

Chapter 10

Eliyakim and Sara

Meanwhile, Eliyakim had followed the forest trails to Avalon, for he had felt an increasing tug within his heart leading back to Sara. She had fulfilled her apprenticeship of seven years with the priestess clans, and was being guided by a powerful vision of things to come.

Sara's training included the mastery of elemental magic, the power of clear seeing, and attunement to the voice of the *Great Mother*. She had also been taught to develop a heightened sensitivity to the subtle currents of energy connecting all things. And so she felt instantly within her the moment that Eliyakim arrived at the shores of Avalon.

She parted the mists to emerge from the mysterious dimension she had become so familiar with, and the two of them met in the forest glades beyond the lake. Unexpectedly shy, they looked at each other across the distance before coming together in a tight embrace. Memories of incarnations past flashed before their eyes, cementing the awakening of love which they had begun to feel for each other.

There was a moment of questioning, for were they not half-brother and sister? But there seemed to be a greater plan at work, which had to do with bloodlines that neither of them fully understood. They recognized they were part of a larger destiny, echoes of which rose deeply within their hearts.

Eliyakim was remembering his visit with the Guardians, when the ancient Manu had told him he was destined to initiate a lineage of kings that would proliferate through the lands of the West. He remembered also the warning he was given that his task would not be easy, that his lineage would pass through great turmoil and shadows, but eventually discover the pure heart of humanity.

As he shared this prophecy with Sara, they were both given a vision of their future. The ancient Manu who had spoken to Eliyakim as a young boy came to them in this vision, and spoke of the magic that had existed within the root race prior to this, their ability to harness the forces of nature in humility and balance, and of the great monuments that had been built.

"This was a time when the leylines and earth grids were being prepared to hold a great vibrational frequency in order to anchor a higher frequency of primordial light. This would allow a new evolutionary impulse to ripple out across the circle of life, including the advent of a root race capable of reaching back to the stars.

"But something went wrong," he continued. "Arrogance and greed took over. Humanity came to confuse the infinite power of the *Great Mother* with the petty powers inherent within the personal self. In your efforts to control the forces of life, you sought to manipulate and enslave the elemental spirits of nature, including crystalline forces that represent the bones of the ancient dragons."

"Many of the wise ones saw what was coming and tried to warn those who sought to arrogantly manipulate these elemental forces. But the warnings fell on deaf ears. The balance of the Earth was lost. She cracked open and entire continents vanished into the sea. Great devastation spread across the land, and millions of species went extinct. Your own species lost much of its genetic potential as the few remaining survivors scattered across the earth, struggling to start anew.

"And thus was your own root race born from the ashes. It was determined that humanity was not yet ready to channel the immense powers of creation, that a greater wisdom and balance was required before your creative powers could be restored to you. You were offered the tree of knowledge so you could learn discernment and wisdom, for only then could the magical powers of the tree of life be responsibly used.

"Your race is still lost in a sea of darkness and fear. Were you to continue along this trajectory you would experience yet another collapse of the earth grids and yet another cataclysmic destruction at the end of your current cycle of *yugas.*

"Your current root race has been exploring a path of reason. This is so you can learn about the law of consequences, or karma, and thus learn wisdom. But reason without magic, or without hope, is dull and stultifying, and your species has descended into a heavy stupor. You have disconnected even further from the quiet whispers of your inner soul.

"It is time for magic to return. It is time to join the magic of the soul with the power of the mind, so that your collective heart may once again open to the deep compassion and exquisite rhythms of nature. It is time for the dragon riders to return now, those among you who have joined heart, mind and soul, who can reach beyond the darkness of this age to harness the winds of new birth."

The Manu looked intently at Eliyakim and Sara. "Your task together is to birth a lineage of kings who are capable of riding the dragons, who can bring back magic to their people. A king is steward of the land. When the heart of a king is corrupt, the people suffer, and so does the Earth. When the heart of a king is open, there is healing and renewal within the land."

"Do you understand this, my children? Hearts can only truly be open when subconscious traumas have been cleared. And this is why you have been chosen for this task. Your father Issa wrestled with the shadows of this age, and conquered his own heart. Your mothers became women of power and grace, aligned with the voice of the *Great Mother*. They have journeyed into the underworld and come back reborn.

"There is no guarantee of success, but your genetics are clear enough that perhaps your descendants can turn the rising tide of darkness. Your siblings are involved in this great work as well, as events will soon reveal."

Chapter 11

Inner Earth

There are things the human personality is still shy to speak about. Although I have lived enough years to fill many ordinary lifetimes, and will likely remain on this earth for countless more, human love has not been part of my path. I suppose my task has been different, and I have never regretted any of it.

But I have wondered at times how it would be to love a man in the way I have seen with my parents, and with each of my brothers. Perhaps when the new race has been established in times to come, there will be space for that too. Meanwhile, it is enough to feel the vast presence of Aisha within me, in her incarnation as a planetary soul, and to feel the whispers of so much life and beauty waiting to be birthed!

Eliyakim and Sara journeyed back together to the gnostic community in France where they had first met. Sara had seen into the future, and recognized that her *Cathar* community faced grave danger at the hands of those who claimed to be followers of Issa. It was her task to prepare them so that when their time came to depart this earth, they would do so with serenity and joy.

Some of them chose to enter Inner Earth dimensions, as the Tuatha de Danann had learned to do. Eliyakim and Sara found that together they could use the power of the dragons to create a doorway into these worlds, as the priestesses of Avalon had also accomplished with their mystical isle. Here they were able to forge links with hundreds of tribes and nations across the earth who had also made their ascension into a higher vibrational world while descending into the etheric body of the earth.

Once the doorway was open, however, Sara and Eliyakim chose to remain in third density, for they remembered the purpose they had come for, and knew they were still needed in the world of men. Four children were birthed through them, each of them destined to create a lineage of kings.

It may surprise many of you reading this manuscript to know how prevalent inner earth civilizations have been throughout the ages. Your planet, just like your own human bodies, has etheric, astral and causal realms which interweave together. Many of the *fae* worlds, such as the Tuatha de Danaan, exist within the etheric dimensions. There are tunnels and networks of communication between them.

Species that have become extinct within the surface worlds continue to thrive here.

Others, such as *Agartha* and *Shambala*, exist within the astral realms, usually found deeper within the body of the Earth. This is the realm, sometimes known as the *Halls of Amenti*, which ascended and cosmic masters inhabit. There are doorways here that open to other planets within this solar system, and also across to other star nations.

And then finally, at the very core of the earth, is a causal realm, a repository of *akashic* knowledge and genetic potential which is directly linked to the heart of this galaxy, and to the *mother stars* of other galaxies across the vast universe.

This is where Aisha has made her home, along with the ancient ones. The *Lords of Time* inhabit this dimension as well, for theirs is the responsibility to support the evolution of all worlds that exist within the thirteen realms of creation, and to make choices that lead to the creation of future timelines. Together, they came to represent the Soul of the Earth.

Time passes differently in each of these realms. If you have wondered how I have lived so many hundreds of years in the same body, or why I can move so easily across time and space, it is because my bodies have attuned to this causal dimension of *Mother Earth*, from which future root races will emerge in the fullness of time.

Chapter 12

The Seventh Initiation

I have hardly spoken at all about the two people who have been most important to me, as well as to this story. I suppose that is the way with stories, you put your foot down in the river and you never know where it is going to take you, and sometimes you leave out pieces you should really have started with!

Everything that I have learned of human love I have learned from my parents – their endless devotion to each other and their children, their total commitment to the task given them, their absolute surrender to the river of life! I could write an entire book about their incredible travels, the stories they told us, and our adventures together!

So how could I not respond when *Great Mother* invited me to step down from fields of starlight that were my home, and join their family! It is thought sometimes that parents choose their children, but it is always a mutual choice, and I could not have come to this Earth embodying the fulness of my being were it not for the purity and power of their own consciousness.

Mirjan had continued her apprenticeship with Aisha during the time that Issa and my brothers were away on their travels. The three of us became inseparable as we began to understand our roles in the evolutionary plan. As Aisha continued to merge deeper within the planetary soul, she needed Mirjan to remain in human form to serve as a bridge. My own task then was to walk across this bridge, join the collective consciousness of humanity, and become the seed for a new tree of life.

It was recognized that in the fulness of time Mirjan would need to take the rainbow body, along with Issa, in such a way that they could continue to hold a physical presence across intervening centuries until the Age of Light had been fully anchored.

The *Cosmic Mother* had also told us that unlike previous ages, when the Earth went through alternating cycles of destruction and creation, darkness and light, she was now ready for her Seventh Initiation, an initiation that would instantly ripple out across all galactic dimensions of a single organic multiverse, entering a continuous spiral of ascending light, with involution and evolution becoming a single impulse of creator consciousness mirrored within the fields of creation.

Chapter 13

Dreams

My mother and I were in our dreaming cave, where we occasionally would go to look for guidance and meet with Aisha. That night I had a dream in which a number of prisoners had been sentenced to death, and were to be executed. Just before their execution they were granted the gift of immortality by a capricious god. And so every day for the rest of their lives they would be taken out into the courtyard to be executed, after which they would be returned to the safety of their cells.

The dream somehow highlighted for me the pointless existence of most of humanity. Many people are dead already but do not know it. They are too afraid to die, and yet too afraid to live. They have entered a treadmill of existential suffering from which there is no hope of escape.

In their case, the idea of immortality had become a curse, and these unfortunate men and women yearned to be lifted out from their endless cycle of pointless existence. I recognized that the dream reflected an entire root race of humanity who were trapped in a treadmill of the mind, where a narrow band of perception, and especially a cultural conditioning around the afterlife, has kept them chained in a slow dance of death.

Humanity was trapped in a false dance of immortality, where the safety of tomorrow became more important than living each moment today, where they were afraid to exchange the insecurity of the known for the security of the unknown, where the fear of death became a fear of life, where people died slowly each moment without knowing they were already dead.

People had become slaves of habits, slaves of routine, slaves of perception that never carried far. They had become slaves to ideas of progress or ideas of religion, ideas of intelligence and self-importance that froze the heart and killed the soul.

I had another dream the following night, where I encountered an old woman by the roadside, encrusted with years, wrapped in stories of pain. She appeared to be one of the living shadows, and I wanted to take her into my arms and breathe vitality into her stiffened form. But she was infused with self-loathing, and resisted any touch or connection. As I sensed the awakening of my inner dragon, a tremendous blaze surged forth from within me, enveloping her heart.

The shell enclosing her cracked open, revealing a fragile young woman emerging from the chrysalis of her old life. Hand in hand, we walked down a forest trail to the edge of a pool, jumping in together. I felt an extraordinary metamorphosis taking place as she opened her heart to the *Great Mother*. She became the embodiment of all those who had hidden their face in darkness out of the pain of too much light.

I had just woken from this dream, and was pondering over its meaning, when I felt the presence of Issa joining us in the cave. He had returned home from his travels, leaving the boys behind in England to pursue their own destinies. There is always something so beautiful and ecstatic about meeting loved ones after a long absence, and even though we never really felt apart anymore, it was a wonderful homecoming.

Aisha then showed up in her own mysterious way. As the four of us came together in celebration, I found myself deeply touched in joy, not only to see my beloved father again, but to know how profoundly each of us sought to break the spell that had been cast on humanity, and how much we longed for these prisoners of the human dream to be set free.

Chapter 14

Timelines

Later that day, as we sat together by the shores of the lake, sharing our stories and eating the picnic meal that had been prepared for us, Chetan Nath came and quietly joined us.

I never ceased to be amazed at how effortlessly both he and Aisha would simply appear when they wished to, and disappear when their work was done. My brothers and I had learned to teleport on occasion, but were not nearly as adept. It required the mastery of elemental forces which we had only partially accomplished as yet.

My brothers and I had always teased our parents about how much better we were at it than either of them. Issa had always responded by saying how much he preferred walking upon the earth than flying over it. He caught my eye now as Chetan Nath showed up, smiling at our secret memory.

For those yet unfamiliar with my mother's earlier manuscripts, Chetan Nath belonged to a lineage of immortal yogis concealed within ancient mountain caves. These enigmatic beings had learned to cross the boundaries of time, and shape the evolutionary journeys of humanity. Chetan Nath had watched over Gautama the Buddha from infancy, later becoming teacher and protector for Issa as well.

He now brought a message from the *nath* lineage, and their newfound alliance with the Guardians. He assured my parents that my brothers would be protected, that they were being guided in a destiny that would shape the future of the western world, and prepare the earth for powerful initiations to come. It had to do with the dragons, and the return of magic to the hearts of men.

He went on to speak of timelines, collective probabilities that shape the future. Humanity seemed trapped within a lower density timeline dictated by the weight of collective karma, hinting at the possibility of great catastrophes while transitioning into the next evolutionary age. However, the *nath* yogis had assumed the task of fashioning an alternative timeline – offering humanity a graceful passage into the new dawn. We each had a role to play in creating this, as Chetan Nath went on to elaborate.

"At the cusp of an age," he continued, "when galactic waves of information and light cascade through your solar system, these new timelines can become activated in such a way that you can effortlessly shift from one stream of possibility into another. It is an intricate play of vibrational frequency and morphogenetic fields, domains which our *rishis* have meticulously explored. Within each particle of matter lie intricate fields of energy, bound into electrons moving across orbits of varying density, a truth your scientists will one day uncover."

"As electrons jump across orbits, quantum leaps take place which defy the passage of linear time. These quantum leaps, experienced within microcosmic realms of atomic existence, are also reflected in macrocosmic dimensions across the universe. It is a holographic unity that connects all things.

"The structure of your own bodies is reflected in the structure of the earth, mirrored upwards in the structure of your solar system, galaxy, and beyond. When the time is ripe for the shift of timelines, triggering a quantum leap of consciousness across your planet, its ripple effect will extend to all aspects of creation above and below. Our own purpose lies in identifying nodes within the flow of time where these alternative timelines can be created, then igniting these pathways with a new evolutionary impulse."

All right, so these may not be the exact words that Chetan Nath used, for these are terms that belong to your age rather than his, but I have taken the liberty of projecting my consciousness into the future, and returning again to my own time, which makes it easy for me to write this story for those who will be reading it in times to come!

Chapter 15

Soul of the Earth

Mirjan asked Aisha then if she could share what it was like to merge with the soul of the Earth.

Aisha flashed her radiant smile, which always had the power to light up everything around her. "Mirjan, my beautiful daughter, you see in front of you the same human form you have always known. But it is more permeable now, and vibrationally different, which means it can shapeshift as required."

"Our sense of identity is built not only from the physical body but from the interaction of five separate bodies, or *koshas*," she went on. "These include the physical, etheric, emotional, mental and causal bodies. In your case, these five bodies, linked together through the earth's magnetic field, provide you with a sense of identity you refer to as human."

"I still experience these same five *koshas,* but in my case, I am able to access a magnetic field extending far beyond the boundaries of the Earth. My *koshas* have therefore become increasingly merged with the *koshas* of *Earth Mother* herself.

Like all things that exist, she is a living being, aware of herself as a conscious entity, experiencing the flow of life much like humans do, but on a much larger scale. The magnetic field that links her five *koshas* extends across the entire solar system, and is receptive to influences far beyond what humans are normally capable of sensing.

"The four lower bodies provide a sense of personal identity, and are associated with thoughts, feelings, memories, and a limited sense of self known as the *ahamkara*. Beyond this, there is a deeper identity known as the soul. This is the realm of the *anandamayakosha*, the fifth body. In your case it is a human soul. In my case, I am increasingly merging with the planetary soul.

I am fully Aisha when I am with you. But I also experience myself as *Mother Earth,* since I have merged with her. This is something many species such as the whales also experience, and all humans are capable of, if they choose to unify with planetary, inter-planetary or galactic magnetic fields. You are each capable of experiencing yourself not only as human, but as planetary, solar and galactic entities as well.

"Indeed, as you learn to work with larger electrical and magnetic fields, you can project yourself into any aspect of creation you wish, and experience that identity as your own."

We allowed ourselves to be impacted by her words. "Tell us more about being the Earth," I asked Aisha after some moments of silence. "Do you experience all species of life as part of yourself?"

Aisha took some time to ponder my question. "I can project my consciousness into whatever form of life I wish to understand," she said. "But not always on a conscious level. "My human form, like yours, is composed of many species functioning as one, including all sorts of bacteria which eventually transform into strands of DNA within each of the cells. But I am not conscious of this unless I choose to be.

"It is the same with my earth form. As I merge with the soul of the earth, I become aware of endless species of life permeating the worlds of nature. I also become aware of functional systems within her body. For instance, just as humans experience the circulation of blood through veins and arteries, so am I learning to experience the circulation of water through rivers and mountain lakes, out across oceans and returning as clouds on a sunny day to come down again as rain.

"But again, I may not be aware of this unless I choose to be. Just like in human form, the majority of these functions are automatic, performed by elemental spirits whose task is to make things grow, regulate the balance of all things, and transmute illness when required. The work of these elemental spirits usually takes place below the surface of conscious awareness.

"On a conscious level, I do experience her thoughts and feelings, and her memories as a soul. *Mother Earth* has an astral body, just like humans do, and experiences a personal identity composed of thoughts and feelings independent of the various species that reside within her. I have access to this, and can travel through dreamtime dimensions with her when I choose to. I also experience her within my causal body, for I experience myself now as both a human soul and a planetary soul.

"This is an onward evolutionary journey. The soul is a holographic entity, and once free from the idea of being fixed in nature, we can experience ourselves as trees or birds or whales or animals, or as planets, stars and galaxies. The soul is simply a unit of consciousness, a reflection of the One Spirit that moves through all things, and can take whatever identity it chooses within the play of consciousness. This is what humanity is evolving towards, and this is what you, Elmira, are here to activate within the collective field of humanity."

Chapter 16

Stagnation

Meanwhile, Mirjan was curious about the dragons, and the age of magic which Chetan Nath had referred to, and asked Aisha if she could share more about this from her perspective.

"Yes indeed," she smiled again. "Nothing would exist without the dragons. Remember when we talked about the *tattwas*, and how all the dimensions of creation come into being from the primordial presence of Shiva and Shakti? Dragons are elemental spirits operating within highly refined fields of universal plasma which make this possible. They are inter-dimensional beings whose great work is to create portals for the unfoldment of life."

"Forget for a moment their mythological status as fire-breathing monsters with scaled bodies and mighty wings. This image symbolizes their power, but their activity is actually much more subtle. There are lines of force which link all dimensions together, a network of electrical and magnetic forces through which the intent of the *Great Mother* can be manifested.

"They represent the elemental forces of fire, earth, water and air. When these forces are rightly understood and properly harnessed, the creative power of the *Great Mother* can be expressed, and you enter the realm of magic. This is how the priestesses of Avalon could create the realm of

Avalon. This is how fairy kingdoms and devas can bring into manifestation species of life never before seen.

"As you know, there are subtle etheric vortexes and channels that operate through your human bodies, known as *chakras, nadis,* and *meridians.* When *kundalini* energies move through these channels, energy and information travels across dimensions of matter to provide the potential for new creation.

"*Mother Earth* has her own network of chakras and meridians, which are known as *ley lines* or *dragon lines.* When kundalini energies flow freely through them, etheric elementals and nature spirits become highly responsive to the will of the *Mother,* and the balance of life can be held easily and joyfully.

"But when these vortexes are blocked, as often happens in response to human aggression, apathy or fear, the forces of life become stagnant, and the vibrational density of matter becomes too heavy for the nature spirits to easily work with.

"Many of the nature spirits have retreated into the shadows, and the magic of the earth realms has therefore been lost. Where there is magic, there is beauty and creativity. Where there is magic, there is a natural flow within the web of life. This is the magic that must be restored now if humanity is to survive the Great Shift, and fulfil its role within the evolutionary plan.

"What happens when water has been stopped behind a dam for too long? It becomes stagnant, and seeks to break through. There is an impulse long held within the energy body of the earth which now seeks to break through. It can happen with destructive force, or it can happen in a manner that is relatively graceful. This is the choice that humanity faces now, the two timelines that Chetan Nath has spoken about."

Chapter 17

Dragon Riders

It was Issa's turn now. "Tell us more about the dragon lines then. How is it possible to restore the flow of life when it has been broken, or dammed up too long?"

"There are 12 *nadis* that move across the earth," responded Aisha. "These *nadis,* or *ley lines,* represent a pathway for elemental dragons existing deep within the earth to interact with surface kingdoms. They correspond with the twelve meridians, and the twelve chakras that link physical and subtle dimensions within your own bodies."

"But I've always assumed there were seven chakras. Where did these other five suddenly come from?" interrupted Issa.

"True, there are seven major chakras existing within the *pranamayakosha,* or etheric body. But there are also gateways at varying distances above the head, which connect the five koshas with each other, all the way up to the *anandamayakosha,* or soul body. A fully integrated human being thus functions within a 12-chakra system, just like *Mother Earth* does, and just like the solar system itself with its 12 planetary vortexes, or homes.

"So restoring the power of the dragons is about restoring the flow of energy through the dragon lines. As this happens, the *rainbow serpent,* as she is known in some traditions, comes alive, and a *rainbow bridge* can be built between our planetary system and galactic sources beyond. Your role as a human species is to become the voluntary nervous system of *Mother Earth*, along with the whale species, to serve as a portal through which she can communicate instantaneously across physical dimensions."

Aisha's eyes sobered as a look of concern flashed across her beautiful face. "In times to come, you will see layers of pollution that will greatly restrict the flow of dragon power across the earth," she went on. "There will be physical pollution, as toxic chemical wastes spread across your atmosphere and the precious oceans. There will be electronic smog as technological devices obscure your etheric networks. There will even be nuclear pollution as destructive powers within the atom are released through weapons of war."

"And then of course there is all the mental pollution you have carried for generations based on roles you have played as aggressor or victim, superior or inferior, sinner or saint. This too keeps you trapped in a timeline of insecurity and fear.

"If you wish to activate the second timeline you will need to reverse this pollution. You will need to join your energies with the sacred energies of the earth in order to initiate a healing process. You will need to work with the elemental kingdoms to restore balance within the dragon lines, and to activate higher vibrational grids capable of holding the frequencies of a new earth consciousness.

"There will come many to this earth in response to this need. They will learn to combine external technologies with inner technologies operating through the power of the heart. They will use the healing power of sound, and the alchemical power of gold, to nourish the etheric body of the Earth. They will learn to work with whales and the nature kingdoms to awaken akashic memories held within waters of the earth, and connect with great oceans beyond.

"These will become known in times to come as children of magic, the *dragon riders.*"

Chapter 18

Akashic Records

All right, so this is an older Elmira now. I have no trouble moving to different periods within my own memory, but since my memories are not limited to a flow of linear time, I realize it must be a little confusing to those of you who are reading this far into my future.

Time moves differently in different dimensions of consciousness. Dragons inhabit all dimensions of space and time, for their essential task is to provide a matrix for the creation of worlds. They rest in between cycles, and emerge again when it's time for a shift.

Most humans operate within a single dimension of space and therefore a single dimension of time. This is generally known as third-dimensional reality, within which time is generally thought to move like an arrow from past to future. Human nervous systems are currently designed so that the flow of linear time is the only way reality can be experienced.

Fae races, such as the Tuatha de Danann, are capable of operating within at least two dimensions of space, and time for them moves more slowly. There are other species on earth that are even more multi-dimensional. Some of them are considered to be mythical, like the unicorns. Others would appear to be physical to you, like the great whales.

Would it surprise you to know that humpback whales have the most complex nervous systems on your planet? If complexity is how you measure greatness, then indeed they are the most advanced species on this earth. They are multi-dimensional, meaning that they simultaneously inhabit many different realities.

Water imprints memory, and provides a link to non-physical dimensions which are etheric in nature. Whales in the ocean are bathed in a field of memory which extends back to the beginnings of life on this planet, and extends out into galactic realms as well. They know how to read this memory, these akashic records.

Akashic records are imprinted within akasha, or fields of ether. Since their experience of time is multi-dimensional however, the memories of these extraordinary beings extend not just into the past but also into the future. If you are willing to learn, they can teach you how you also can do so.

I learned to swim in glacial waters before I learned to walk. The water spirits taught me how to access my memories, and to maintain a continuity between dimensions just like the whales do. I learned to follow my own footsteps across worlds that are thinly separated from each other.

These abilities will someday become natural to all humans. You can begin by focusing on a chakra a short distance behind the back of your head, which is physiologically the space that whales breathe from. Become empty, and invite them to teach you.

In human physiology, this space can be considered as an emerging chakra, a vortex that links you spherically across dimensions. As you develop a mastery of this *whale chakra*, you can learn to merge with aspects of reality yet unknown, move across non-linear dimensions of time, and even join with planetary and galactic levels of soul.

Chapter 19

Morphogenetic Fields

We spoke earlier about *akasha*, the etheric fields which hold memories from the past. These fields not only hold memories, however, but also shape forms and potentialities for the future. In this case they are known as *morphogenetic fields*.

Morphogenetic fields are non-physical informational blueprints that underpin and guide all biological forms, behaviors and patterns in nature. They are creator fields, emanating from templates held within the consciousness of our planet, operating through the activity of nature spirits, focused within genetic pathways known as DNA, to evolve various species on this earth.

They are like memory banks, accumulating experiences and knowledge from generations past, influencing the present, and guiding the unfolding of future evolution.

These fields are not limited by space and time, and can therefore transmit themselves across vast galactic space. The blueprint for any species that has ever existed continues to exist within the akashic field of the planet that birthed them. This blueprint can be invited by the consciousness of any other planet in any other sector of the galaxy, and even across to vast networks of other galaxies, to propagate there.

Your scientists have developed a mistaken idea of evolution, that life evolves accidentally or by chance from pre-existing forms of life. No, each planetary entity chooses precisely what forms she wishes to incarnate within her body, and assigns etheric beings known as *devas*, or nature spirits, to watch over them, supporting a balance between different species to create a functional web of life.

Each species has its own morphogenetic grid. These grids interact with each other, balancing and enhancing each other to support the optimum number and distribution of various species on your planet.

Thus, you have fewer tigers than the deer they feed upon, and multiple kinds of grasses for deer to graze on. You have pollinators such as bees to support a profusion of flowering plants. You have scavengers to feed off dead creatures, and bugs that help them return back to the soil.

All this happens effortlessly through the activity of morphogenetic fields, which make subtle adjustments when required to compensate for inevitable changes that follow the cycles and seasons of life.

Your current human species, through its arrogant assumption that it exists outside this web of life, and is born to dominate the rest of creation, has become an existential threat to balance of life. *Mother Earth* tolerates this, because she recognizes the potential within you, and understands that you are still exhibiting collectively the immaturity of youth.

But this is why my own task has become so urgent. Unless your current root race comes into balance soon, it can very quickly destroy the balance of life, and set back the evolutionary purpose of our beautiful planet by millions of years.

Chapter 20

Planetary Hierarchies

Morphogenetic fields not only shape the physical traits of various species on earth, but also behavioral traits. The mating dance of a peacock, the migration of animals across vast distances, the protective instincts of a mother bear protecting her cubs, are also inherited from generation to generation, contributing to the well-being of these species.

Unfortunately, your current human species, operating from an excessive need to take from the balance of life, without the ability or willingness to give back, has created a cancer within itself and upon the earth. This has created the morphogenetic field of *duality*, symbolized by the *tree of knowledge*. This now needs to be balanced by the *tree of life*.

By recognizing how this field of duality has subconsciously affected your thoughts, feelings and behaviors, and how this affects the interconnectedness of all things, you can achieve a more thoughtful and responsible relationship with the children of the earth, based on greater compassion, understanding and harmony. You can grow into a future that benefits both your own species and the natural world.

The tree of life extends through many dimensions. There are morphogenetic fields existing within primordial dimensions, that have to do with the dance of shiva with shakti. As we step down into the matrix of space and time, another morphogenetic field expresses itself as the intent of the *Mother*, moving through long eons of time, shaping the conditions where life can be experienced.

There is then a morphogenetic field that shaped worlds through sacred geometry. There are Founder species within these worlds, sometimes known as the Elohim, and linked with a number of star systems beyond your own, who are capable of holding a unified consciousness within the field of evolving matter.

These first three levels of morphogenesis are linked with the process of Winvolution, the intent of the *Great Mother* becoming externalized across endless dimensions of time and space. Now begins a process of evolution, a great profusion of life birthed on planetary spheres of varying density across the universe. This eventually resulted in the density of matter, giving rise to a multitude of physical life forms, each with its own morphogenetic field.

In *Mirjan Daughter of the Moon*, my mother has referred to the 44 *tattwas* as taught to her by Aisha. I won't repeat these teachings, except to say that the creation of physical matter has been the very last tattwa in the descent of cosmic consciousness. It is also where the potential exits for the greatest embodiment of creator consciousness. This is why *Mother Earth* has chosen to keep humans around, even with all their unruliness. This is what future root races of humanity will reveal.

Chapter 21

Four Faces of the Mother

The four hierarchical morphogenetic fields reflect the four faces of the *Mother* in her mighty act of cosmic creation. There is *Maheshwari*, the primordial aspect of the *Mother* that has always existed beyond the matrix of time and space, before worlds and dimensions were created. She stands apart and alone, potential energy existing within all things, endlessly dancing with Shiva as movement within stillness, stillness within movement.

Then there is *Mahakali*, the wild aspect of the *Mother*, rippling across the veils of maya to create the matrix of the universe. Time and space are the mysterious components of this matrix, moving differently through descending *tattwas* and dimensions. Filaments of plasma are imprinted with the creative will of *Mahakali* to initiate a dream that will one day give rise to galaxies, stars and endless varieties of planetary life.

Mahasaraswati comes along then, creating fields of sacred geometry capable of interacting with magnetic fields to initiate the templates of life. There are still no physical forms, only an endless array of morphogenetic fields held within the mind of *Great Mother Saraswati*.

And then finally, there is the act of physical creation. The Goddess *Mahalakshmi* moves across space and time in a profusion of diversity and beauty, morphogenetic fields exploding into stars and galaxies, followed by a range of astral, etheric and material worlds, mirrored within each other but also separated within time and space.

This final act of creation represents what your scientists have called the Big Bang. The will of the *Mother* can now be manifested through interacting fields of energy and matter to give rise to the building blocks of physical reality. Life is created and evolves, mind is created and evolves, until finally, with the birth of galactic humans, the first seeds of a self-reflective consciousness begin to sprout.

This is where you are today. The density of physical matter is designed one day to contain and reflect the entire consciousness of the *Great Mother*. It was not originally intended that humans descend into a field of duality, but with the advent of mind and self-reflective consciousness, this became an intervening phase.

As you build the *tree of life*, however, you will learn to find your way out from the field of duality. Involution and evolution will become a single act of creative expression, expressing the will of the *Great Mother* in every act of physical movement. You will become the face of the *Mother*, her eyes and ears, her hands and feet, just as I now experience within myself.

Chapter 22

Quantum Shift

Most of you reading this will soon be experiencing waves of galactic energy pouring in. Mystic researchers of your time refers to cosmic electricity infiltrating the five koshas of your planetary existence, initiating an event known as the *three days of darkness* that will become the birthing passage to a new world.

Your astrophysicists speak of galactic superwaves emanating from the center of your galaxy, shortly reaching the edge of your solar system, and creating a chain reaction across inter-planetary space. Your geologists talk about the imminent reversal of your geomagnetic field and what this could mean for life on the earth.

The signs are clear. You don't need me to tell you what your mystics and prophets have already told you. But sometimes it is easy to ignore voices that are much too close, and turn a blind eye to things that are much too obvious.

You will not experience an extinction event. My consciousness holds all probabilities of your future, and I can tell you with certainty that the winter you currently face will be followed by a springtime of renewal and hope. There is nothing to fear. The great shift your mystics and prophets have seen is imminent. The only question is how graciously and fearlessly you are willing to step into your own rebirth.

In my own experience of moving between dimensions, there is usually a change in the perception of time, followed by a moment of singularity. In other words, the gap between significant events grows exponentially smaller, followed by a quantum shift. The faster and more intense the waves of contraction, the closer you are to the moment of birth.

Your physicists have come to believe that quantum shifts only take place on subatomic levels of reality. But this is not so. These shifts take place on macrocosmic levels also, although separated by longer distances in linear time.

Another interesting aspect of quantum fields is that when a quantum shift takes place within one dimension of reality, it has the potential to ripple out instantly across all dimensions of time and space.

Creation did not begin with a Big Bang. Nor did it end there. Creation happens in endless cycles from the centers of galaxies, and through ripples of consciousness emanating out across multiple dimensions during times of quantum shift.

And this is what you are due to experience soon. A moment of birth is imminent. The new world that you are moving towards already exists. What you are due to experience in linear time has already been created in consciousness. As your human consciousness expands to embrace this potential, that timeline then becomes manifest in linear history.

To understand more about what I am saying here, let me take you back into the story of your past.

Chapter 23

Dwapara Yuga

Those of you reading this in the early 21st century have been conditioned to believe that yours is the most advanced civilization that ever walked this earth. You have moved from an agrarian age into an industrial age into an electronic age that even borders on the use of digitally enhanced artificial intelligence.

Your outer technologies have indeed advanced. But what does this have to do with cultural advancement or spiritual advancement, or even with the experience of contentment or fulfilment in life? You have polluted your home with the waste products of a diseased world, and filled your etheric bodies with electronic signals too discordant to sense the subtle whispers of a more luminous world.

Contrast this with civilizations that existed in earlier cycles of time. You have heard of the Lemurian Age, where language did not exist because all communication was telepathic, where machinery was unknown because anything required could be created directly from the ethers.

Your ancient histories also speak of an Atlantean Age where sound was used to move massive blocks of stone, or elemental spirits participated in the creation of beautiful gardens and cities. There were many dragon riders in those times, because you had learned to harness the power of elemental forces to create harmony and goodness.

But then, as each of these civilizations went through their own cycles of growth and decay, all this changed. The same tendencies for arrogance and greed that plagued many galactic races began to infiltrate the Atlantean world, which finally ended in a great cataclysm 12,000 years ago. In a single day, entire continents were sunk, while new land masses emerged from the ocean.

Each Age is associated with a different vibrational frequency and a different physical density. Your own age began with the sinking of Atlantis during the last phase of a *dwapara yuga*. As you descended into *kali yuga*, you began to experience a denser vibrational frequency, removing your ability to manipulate elemental forces as you had learned to do in Atlantis.

Those of you in the 21st century should know that the *kali yuga* has now ended, and that you are entering the first phase of the next *dwapara yuga*. This is an age of energy. It began with the splitting of the atom. "Lo, I am become death incarnate, destroyer of worlds," announced the inventor of this technology.

If the *kali yuga* was an age of inertia, the *dwapara yuga* is an age where new choices become possible, and alternate timelines become available. It is the moment when elder dragons awaken from their slumber and higher frequencies of galactic light enter your evolutionary stream.

Your movement from the *dwapara yuga* to *kali yuga* was accompanied by massive waves of destruction and death. But there were a few, including some of the Guardians that we met, who were able to surf the power of those same waves to achieve their ascension.

In this age, as you make the shift, a new timeline is being created that will not require cataclysmic events. There is a mechanism, which I will describe later in this manuscript, which will help ease the transition. Each will be required to make a choice, however.

As I hinted before, dragons are doorkeepers between dimensions, guardians of high magic, whose task is to create alternate timelines when needed. But there is a test that each person alive will need to pass through. During the days of Atlantis, the power of the dragons was abused and manipulated for selfish ends, which led eventually to the destruction of a great civilization.

This will not be allowed again. The dragons will test your hearts and your secret intentions. "Do you serve the *Mother?*" is the question you will each have to answer for yourselves.

Chapter 24

Guild of Merlins

Let us go back now to the time of my brothers, and the return of magic to the land. I left you with the guild of merlins that Hiranya and Arwyn had founded, which soon began to attract a great number of men and women who yearned for deeper connection with the natural world.

As humans entered deeper into the *kali yuga*, they found that their senses had diminished, and they no longer had the capacity to experience the vitality and power of the nature realms. And so teachers emerged from the plant kingdoms whose task was to help these students with expanding their sensory perceptions.

Fly agaric fairies were one line of nature spirits who volunteered to create a bridge between human and *fae*. During nights when the moon was full, and at times of the year when veils became thin, Hiranya and Arwyn would lead their students in special ceremonies where they would partake of a brew made from sun-dried mushrooms infused with starlight.

Red caps spotted with white, fly agaric mushrooms are toxic for most humans. But when dried and properly prepared, they allowed Hiranya's merlins to walk through the veil between worlds, open their senses to the enchantment of nature, and learn to communicate with subtle fields of intelligence invisible to most people.

There are many tribes of higher-dimensional humans, or *sidhe*, associated with the worlds of nature. Otherwise known as *elves*, they occupy a range of frequencies, some of them closer to physical dimensions, others further away. The Tuatha de Danann existed close to the human range, and were therefore easy to communicate with, although permission was first required from an elder within the tribe.

There are also nature spirits linked with trees, animals, mountains, streams, gardens and forests. These are known as fairies, elementals, pixies, leprechauns, devas, gnomes, or nature spirits. They too are part of the natural cycle of all things, and are in constant communication with the etheric body of the earth. Without them the breath of life could not flow freely. Trees could not grow, species could not communicate with each other, and the harmony of nature would be broken.

Merlins would be trained to expand their sense perceptions so they could gradually begin to communicate with all forms of life, physical as well as etheric, harmonizing and balancing, even learning to enter the astral worlds where humans normally transfer their consciousness when the physical body drops away at death. They also learned to energize circles of stone in order to enhance and stabilize energy currents across the earth.

As the community of druids continued to grow, communion with the nature kingdoms became a weekly sacrament. Hiranya would offer them cakes of dried agaric mushroom to activate the inner eye, while his elven wife Arwyn offered precious elixirs crafted from the essence of flowers and stones, so they could travel safely through these expanded worlds.

Once they had participated in this communion, the druids would lie down within portals of stone, heads facing towards the center, listening to guidance from the worlds of nature. It was not easy at first, for after centuries of being ignored and persecuted, many elemental spirits had withdrawn themselves from the world of humans.

But as the merlins learned to cross between dimensions, and open the doors of perception, a profound transformation was set into motion. With each step taken in the pursuit of ancient wisdom, the bonds of trust, once shattered, began to mend like a tapestry of fate being carefully rewoven.

Soon came a time when the doors of perception were cleansed enough, and the nervous system refined enough, that the very presence of the merlins, and their spoken intention, was enough to open the doorways, and the mushrooms were no longer required. It is not wise to create a dependence on anything external, not even this most sacred of medicines.

Over the years, as the veil between the worlds became thinner, a fresh awakening swept across the land like a gentle breeze of enchantment. Nature herself seemed to respond to the return of forgotten knowledge. Crops flourished, and the forests hummed with life as animals and birds returned to take their place in the symphony of existence.

Perhaps the most extraordinary change was the fairies and elemental spirits emerging from the shadows, their ethereal presence gracing the realms of humanity once more. With mischievous laughter and benevolent curiosity, they extended a graceful hand towards humankind, bridging the chasm that had separated them for so long.

The world seemed to shimmer with possibilities and the promise of harmonious coexistence. The guild of druids was filled with the delighted laughter of merlins, as each of them awakened the elemental aspect of their own nature, the inner child. As they reached across the boundaries of perception, they discovered that the universe was indeed woven from threads of inter-connectedness.

In this tapestry of renewal, the enchanting dance of cosmic harmony played on, leaving none untouched by the power of rediscovered magic. As they embraced the realm of undiscovered senses, the land became once again a realm of mystical splendor.

Physicality

All right, so I hope it is becoming clear to you now that what we call magic is simply the ability to recognize and co-operate with the elemental forces of nature, who in turn know how to control and regulate the earth's magnetic fields.

The elder dragons, also known as the *elohim*, work with vast filaments of plasma, creating wormholes within cosmic electrical fields which condense to form magnetic fields. Magnetic fields shape morphogenetic fields, which in turn give rise to varying densities and dimensions of reality. Ultimately, as magnetic fields continue to condense, physical universes are created, with planets and star systems such as your own.

What you call the physical world is nothing but a consensus reality held within the collective consciousness of humanity. It is shaped by morphogenetic fields held within the mind of creation. Dragon riders are those who can enter the mind of the elder dragons and create alternate timelines within an existing consensus reality. This is how the realm of Avalon, and the otherworld of the Tuatha de Danann came into being.

Your own world has become fixed in what you call *linear time*. As long as there is freedom and diversity of culture, thought and experience, there is a wide range of movement within which many realities and timelines can simultaneously exist. Unfortunately, through fixed expressions of science, philosophy, and religion, your world has become increasingly homogenized, increasingly stuck in a narrow expression of truth, a frozen morphogenetic field known as *consensus reality*.

Within the grand tapestry of existence, what many perceive as the physical world is, in truth, a wondrous mirage woven within the ethereal realm of collective consciousness. Within the higher realms of the human mind, a multitude of morphogenetic fields are braided together to sculpt the fabric of time and space. Over the course of time, however, due to limiting belief systems, your consensus reality has become fixed and stunted.

The difference between magical realities and fixed realities has to do with how many layers of morphogenetic fields can be incorporated within your belief system and within your energy bodies. When multiple morphogenetic fields can be seamlessly woven together, this manifests as higher densities of existence, or higher dimensional realities. As reality becomes increasingly fixed through forced expressions of consensual thought, it results in the tasteless flavorless world that Aisha refers to as *third density*.

Within your own dimension of time, you may have noticed that when you are in a creative flow, your experience of time speeds up, and there is room for synchronicity. When you fall into familiar routines and fixed states of mind, time seems to crawl, and boredom sets in.

Your experience of time also changes when you move across to other dimensions or densities. In the *fae* worlds for instance, time moves at a very different pace than it does for humans living in the physical world. There are innumerable stories of those who have crossed over into these realms, and returned to find that hundreds of years have passed in their absence.

Nature spirits operate within a dimension that is subtler than the physical worlds, and therefore work within a different structure of time. They have access to akashic records, which are the morphogenetic fields of new creation, and therefore have the capacity not only to support existing species of physical life, but also to bring entirely new species into existence.

Chapter 26

Magnetic Fields

This brings us back to magnetic fields. Garden spirits and fairies strengthen the magnetic fields around plants so they grow faster and more abundantly. The same goes for animals and birds. Each species of life has an overlighting deva, which interacts with the deva of every other species within an ecosystem, eventually creating a functional web of life.

The problem with humans is that there is not one single overlighting deva regulating your species. *Mother Earth*, in her quest for a species capable of bridging earth and sky, has allowed each individual human an attribute of free will, the power to control in a limited way the destinies of other species on the Earth. This has created an element of chaos on earth.

Hiranya's merlins had learned to charge their etheric body with a great deal of magnetism, and were therefore capable of regulating the passage of time, communicate across dimensions, access subtle morphogenetic fields, and create alternate timelines. Their very presence could reach across dimensions to bring fertility and harmony to the earth.

When there is harmony within the web of life, plasma fields extend to the etheric body of the Earth, communicating with elemental forces which control lightning and patterns of rainfall across the earth. Jet streams are created which move cloud systems where needed, in order to bring fertility and balance to the land.

Your exercise of free will, rather than contributing to balance, has unfortunately led to a great deal of imbalance upon the earth. This has happened in other ages as well, and *Mother Earth* is capable of correcting this. These corrections take place during times of transition between ages, and the magnetic reversals which typically follow the transition from *dwapara yuga* to *kali yuga,* or from *kali yuga* to *dwapara yuga.*

Those of you who are reading this in the early 21st century will be experiencing a reversal within your lifetimes. Your geomagnetic field is already weakening at an increasingly exponential rate. Although I cannot give you a precise date, expect that the zero point will be achieved shortly after the release of this manuscript into the world.

The last phase of this reversal will happen very quickly. Prophecies from indigenous cultures refer to *three days of darkness,* equivalent to this time of magnetic reversal. Record keepers from these traditions look forward to this event with great hope, yet caution people to go inside their homes and remain still during this moment in time.

This is the moment when a unified human consciousness can be created, resulting in the creation of a single *devic* consciousness representing all of humanity. We will return to this theme, but let us first go back again to the time of the merlins, so you can better understand the choices that lie in front of you.

Chapter 27

Scourge of Christianity

Every time there is an opening in consciousness, something comes along from the realms of the unconscious to resist and challenge this awakening. This seems to an alchemical rule within the experience of duality.

And so it was that just as the merlins had learned to achieve a certain level of balance within the natural world, a new challenge came into existence. In a tragic inversion of everything my father had given his entire life to, it came in the form of what became known during those times as Christianity.

Waves of Roman invaders, carrying the flag of the Roman Catholic Church, streamed into the lands of Britain, conquering the Celtic tribes, destroying the sacred groves, and desecrating the stone altars that had been built to stabilize the telluric currents flowing through the earth.

The *elves* and nature kingdoms, who had been starting to come out of hiding, once again went underground as the order of the ancient druids began to fall apart. Following the renewal of trust between human and *fae* kingdoms, the veil between the physical and etheric worlds had become increasingly thinner. Suddenly, this became threatened.

Once again, during the early centuries following the birth of my father, the winds of change began to blow. Like a tidal wave, this foreign faith swept across the shores of Britain, bringing with it a new way of seeing the world, a different understanding of the divine, and an unmistakable shift in the collective consciousness.

The banner of Christianity, carried by zealous missionaries and determined soldiers, marked the beginning of a profound transformation in the spiritual landscape of Britain. A clash of beliefs became inevitable, as the Christian message sought to supplant the deeply rooted tradition of the Druids.

With the rise of Christianity, the very foundation of magic began to crumble. The wise counsel of the Druids, who once guided the tribes with their profound knowledge of nature's secrets, was now dismissed as sorcery, paganism, and witchcraft. The standing stones, which once served as portals between worlds, were now seen as idols to be destroyed.

The spirits that had danced among the sacred sites retreated into the shadows. The tenuous relationship between humans and the natural world once again became fractured, as the new faith proclaimed dominion over nature rather than unity with it.

A new consensus reality began to replace the old. Those who clung to the old ways were branded as heathens and heretics, facing persecution and death. Hiranya's merlins, who had learned to carry the ancient wisdom, were threatened with oblivion.

In the face of this overwhelming change, pockets of resistance persisted, and the echoes of the ancient magic refused to be silenced entirely. Some sought refuge in remote corners of the land, preserving fragments of ancient knowledge. Others merged aspects of the old ways with the new, seeking a delicate balance between the worlds.

The priestesses of Avalon separated themselves entirely from the external world, continuing their ancient rites in secret, awaiting a time when they could emerge once again. The enchantment of the old ways slowly became a distant memory, obscured by shadows cast by the rising steeples of Christian churches. The realm of magic that had once flourished under the watchful eyes of the Druids, faded into the mists of time, leaving behind only whispers and legends of a bygone era.

Chapter 28

The Grail Kings

Centuries passed. Eliyakim and Sara had departed from their physical bodies, leaving behind a line of descendants who became the lineage holders for the so-called Grail Kings. This title was rooted in the idea that the cup which Issa drank from at his crucifixion contained magical powers, and would provide the owner of this cup dominion over other kings in a war-torn land. The quest for this Holy Grail became a historical theme during endless centuries of regional strife.

The esoteric meaning behind this title was quite different, however. The same word, *graal*, which means *cup*, also means *sacred womb*. It was the sacred womb of Sara, as daughter of Issa and Mari, that would in due time birth a lineage capable of weaving the realm of magic back into the world of men. Eliyakim, son of Issa and Mirjan, carried the genetics representing the 12 galactic tribes, and the two of them were thus given the responsibility of bringing forth the Grail King.

There is a mystery that has been largely forgotten in the Western world. The 12 Hebrew tribes represented earthly races of humanity. Mirjan's shamanic ancestry also incorporated earlier lineages of 12 galactic, or extra-terrestrial tribes. The weaving of magic in the world of men has to do with the integration of DNA from each of these tribes within a new species of humanity. The birth of a new human species at the cusp of the next world age is what the symbolic quest for the holy grail is really about.

It is the dragons who are responsible to create a passage from one world age to the next. It was necessary for elder dragons who had remained dormant during long millennia to now awaken in preparation for this passage, during the magnetic reversal I have spoken about earlier.

This is where Hiranya comes in once again. As one who had allied himself to the world of the *fae,* he had remained within the same physical form for many generations, along with his beautiful wife Arwyn. As a dragon rider, he could harness the power of these dragons, and dream new timelines into existence.

But for this to be accomplished, he needed to work directly with the world of men, through the power of a king who was wedded to the land. The spiritual devotion of the Christian priesthood needed to be merged with the mystical currents of ancient wisdom. It was his task to find somebody within the lineage of kings within whom these two currents could co-exist.

Within the lineage of the Grail Kings, there was one who had allied himself with the power of the dragons. He called himself Uther Pendragon. Hiranya, or *Merlin,* as he was now being called, recognized that it was through Uther that his brother Eliyakim would be reincarnated once again, to become not only a ruler of men but a steward of cosmic energies.

Thus was born one who would become a name whispered through time as King Arthur. Sara incarnated during this time among the priestesses of Avalon as his half-sister Morgaine. It was intended that she become his support and companion, and that together they would restore the age of magic that had been broken. Arwyn, as Lady of the Lake, offered him a magical sword of truth, named Excalibur, which was to be used in service to the Goddess.

However, in a tragic turn of the wheel, Arthur found himself overly influenced by the priests of his time to exile his half-sister, and subsequently marry a staunchly Christian princess named Guenevere. Although Merlin was still able to work the magic of the dragons with him to a certain extent, the end came quickly.

Guenevere found herself having an affair with Arthur's most trusted knight, Launcelot. which broke his heart and affected his ability to maintain his stewardship over the land. Morgaine was imprisoned by the priesthood, and later executed. Arthur himself was manipulated by Guenevere to sever his connection with Merlin and the realms of the *fae*.

In a sad twist of destiny, Arthur was killed by his own son, Mordred, who in his lust for power, had given himself over to the dark side of magic. With the death of Arthur, Hiranya realized that the age of magic was not yet to be. Along with Arwyn, he retreated into the *otherworld,* where they lived their remaining years among the Tuatha de Danann.

Once again, a veil of darkness covered the land. But the age of magic will one day return. Eliyakim, the once and future king, will incarnate again, along with Sara, in order to complete their mission. So will Hiranya and Arwyn. Will they return as individual souls or as a collective expression of these archetypal energies? That story is being written now, and will involve each of you currently reading this manuscript.

Chapter 29

The Saturnian Matrix

Before I move on now to my parents, Issa and Mirjan, and their own role in this great tapestry of renewal, I would first like to make some comments relevant to your current times. I realize I have a tendency to leapfrog across the stream of linear time, and I know this can be sometimes confusing. But I wish for you to understand history in a different way, and confront belief systems that need to be questioned.

History is not a series of events taking place in linear time. It is rather a matrix of possibility, within which various timelines can be played out according to collective choices, vibrational density, and an underlying evolutionary plan.

The destiny of Merlin and King Arthur was to initiate an age of magic and harmony which would have changed the face of human history. Britain was the center of the world at that time. If they had succeeded in their mission, colonial empires would not have arisen. War would no longer be a means for settling disputes. Dominant elites such as the *Illuminati,* along with structures of enslavement currently known as the *Cabal* or *Deep State,* would not have come into power.

Free energy technologies would have proliferated. Ancient wisdom would have been revived. Collective trauma held for millennia within the cellular memory of humanity would have been lifted. You would have passed through the upcoming magnetic reversal in a state of ease and grace.

Alas, that particular experiment ended in failure. But Hiranya and his merlins ensured that the seeds for a future renewal were planted within the memory fields of the earth. Guilds for the training of merlins and dragon riders continued in secrecy. Wisdom keepers around the world continued to carry the ancient knowledge. Whisperers continued to communicate with the *fae*, and with the nature kingdoms. Extraordinary artists, scientists, mystics and seers continued to offer visions of hope.

These visions of hope were planted within energy pathways known as *ley lines* or *dragon lines* to energize the meridian systems of the earth, from whence they could move into a region of the earth known as the *noosphere*. Like pyramids and stone circles in former days, a global grid system was established, along with a set of dimensional portals, to prepare the vibrational frequency of the earth for a quantum shift.

I spoke earlier about history being a matrix of possibility. You are currently ruled by a distorted matrix of power which has become separated from the soul of the earth. I could refer to this as the satanic, malignant or demonic matrix, for I see how hateful and hurtful the power of these subconscious patterns can be.

But I will make an attempt to be kind. It is a template of reality based on the experience of duality, and I will simply call this the *saturnian matrix,* in reference to the confining or retracting qualities of the planet Saturn. This is the matrix that drives the *Deep State*, a small elite with a soulless agenda which has infiltrated your political and banking structures. It is magnetic in nature, and is therefore able to influence collective human thoughts, feelings, moods and memories. Because of its low vibrational frequency however, it will not survive the magnetic reversal.

This is the vision of hope I am referring to. As the distorted matrix disintegrates during the three days of darkness, a new *organic matrix* will be energized, within which the creative power of the collective soul can once again be manifested.

The task ahead will not be easy. Discordant belief systems and distorted patterns of energy have given rise to a prison planet where creativity and diversity has been replaced by false structures of power. Freedom of thought has been eclipsed by monolithic censorship. Expressions of individual and national sovereignty have been replaced with corporate monopolies and military dictatorships.

As you read these words in the early 21st century, know that the time for renewal is at hand. Warrior souls are being invited from across the galaxies, joining with star walkers already present on earth, to tear down the *saturnian matrix* rooted in fear. Dragon riders will move out to create a collective timeline in keeping with the evolutionary plan of *Mother Earth*.

The subsequent collapse of existing structures may appear chaotic for some time, but an age of magic will inevitably follow. A higher-dimensional matrix harmonized with etheric morphogenetic fields is being set up now to replace the third density grid system of your prison planet.

Chapter 30

Christ Consciousness Grid

All right, then. With this background it should become easier for you to understand the specific roles each of us were to play in this evolutionary drama. Issa and Mirjan were given the responsibility of building the higher dimensional matrix, or grid system. As this new grid system became increasingly manifested, it would give Aisha the opportunity to incarnate more deeply through all the *koshas* linked with *Mother Earth*. And then I could fulfil my own task of creating a template for the new human species.

You are currently living in a time when two grid systems are simultaneously operating on the Earth. As I said earlier, the third dimensional grids have become increasingly hijacked by discordant forces seeking to establish total control of human consciousness.

You must understand that intentions have power. A strong intention is capable of permeating the geometries of life all the way from the noosphere where collective belief systems are created and anchored, to the vibrational frequency of matter itself. The focused intention of a few dark magicians was enough to keep this beautiful planet mired in the sticky webs of duality which prevented most of you from truly incarnating as a soul.

The great work of Issa and Mirjan, and for those of you walking in their footsteps, has been to dismantle this matrix, while simultaneously creating a *christ-consciousness grid*. In order to understand how this works, you must understand the deeper laws of alchemy.

You have learned to perceive reality through the lens of duality, which means that the entire universe becomes a dance between forces of good and evil locked in mortal combat. But what happens when your perceptions change, when you begin to see that everything is holographically reflected within everything else? Can you recognize that all these faces of creation are present within your own psyche as well?

Alchemy is not so much about turning lead into gold, which your medieval alchemists were so obsessed about, as recognizing that both lead and gold are already and always present within you. "As above so below. As within so without." Your task then becomes to shift your perceptions of reality until reality itself undergoes a shift.

Do you understand what I am saying? This work requires being able to enter the heart of darkness until all that remains is light. It means to enter the heart of your enemy to discover therein your own face. It means to penetrate the veils of duality recognizing that everything you perceive on the outside is simply a mask of the goddess within.

Once the veils of duality have been penetrated with the light of unified consciousness, new worlds can instantly be created. Duality is not something that belongs to the density of matter so much as a density of mind. Once the veils of the collective subconscious have been parted, the geometries of a new grid system can be anchored.

This is the mystical work that Aisha initiated in her journey to the underworld with the support of Chetan Nath and my parents. It is the same journey each of you must make in order to transmute the collective darkness of this age. You will discover then that what you call *darkness* is simply the womb of creation, the dark soil from which a new world can be born.

Alchemy

In order to understand alchemy you must also begin to question your perceptions of size. How does your perception of reality change when you recognize that the universe is inside you, that all time and space exist within you, that all dimensions of reality are birthed through you?

Once you truly understand this, you will no longer be intimidated by the concept of size. You will understand what it means for Aisha to incarnate as a planet, or for myself to become the Manu of a new root race.

Let me remind you again of Indra's Net, which Aisha has so eloquently described. You can conceive all things within creation as a net of pearls stretching infinitely in all directions. In each weave of this infinite net rests a beautiful pearl. Each of these pearls reflects as well as contains the image of every other pearl.

The metaphor illustrates the interpenetration of all phenomena. Whatever affects one pearl effects them all, because ultimately there is only a single pearl in the entire universe, and each of us is a hologram of that single pearl. The entire universe exists within each one of us.

What if each of you were to experience yourself as a pearl within this Net? Would it matter then whether you identified with a galaxy or a planet, a flower or a human being? The same geometries present in a tiny atom are reflected in the spiral arms of a spinning galaxy; the same soul that can incarnate in a human body can also incarnate within a planetary body.

The problem is that most of you perceive only the physical body of *Mother Earth*. What if you began to perceive her higher bodies? What if you understood that the same five *koshas* that constitute your human self also constitute your planetary self? What if you entered deeply enough into a single cell within your human body to discover an entire universe therein?

Chapter 32

Gaia

There was a time when your language reflected this understanding. You perceived *Mother Earth* as a living system, a single organism with systems and structures much like your own. You personified her, giving her a name that she could respond to. Our people referred to her as *Prithvi*, the Sumerians knew her as *Ninhursag*, the Greeks called her *Gaia*, the Romans named her *Terra*, and the Inka addressed her as *Pachamama*.

In your own time there is an emerging concept known as the *Gaia Hypothesis*, where scientists are beginning to recognize that *Mother Earth* is a living being just like you are, with organs and systems much like your own.

Her skeletal system includes the mountains, rocks and minerals that shape her physical body. Magnetic forces and tectonic activity represent her muscular system. Her circulatory system includes the waters within and around the earth, shaping climate patterns that create clouds and rain, mighty rivers that flow back down to the sea. The waters of the earth are capable of imprinting morphogenetic fields that maintain the balance of life.

Her breath is drawn from solar winds and moves across the face of the earth in gentle breezes and mighty storms. Subtle movements within her tectonic plates reflect the activity of a finely tuned muscular system, sometimes giving rise to violent upheavals and volcanic eruptions.

Trees and plants are the lungs of the earth, and also represent her etheric body, their interlocking root systems linked to memory fields across the earth. Microscopic mycelium and plankton represent her vital force, for without them the chain of life would quickly break down.

Birds and animals reflect a complex symphony within the web of life, each species representing a different note within her emotional body. Your human species has become capable of creating abstract ideas, leading to philosophies and technologies that play a role in shaping the mental body of the earth.

The Earth has an immune system, just as you do, which helps her come back into balance when streams of energy are broken. This has to do with her vibrational frequency, which are harmonics within what your scientists are able to measure as Schuman resonances. These harmonics change as new grid systems are established. This is happening in your times, as many of you are already discovering.

Bacteria and viruses, rather than being unfriendly micro-organisms as many of you imagine, help her maintain the circle of life, taking care of minute functions within her body, while also providing mitochondrial pathways within DNA. Various feedback loops help her return to balance following major climatic changes.

Mother Earth also has a nervous system, much like your own. Humanity functions as her left brain, while cetaceans represent her right brain. Your interactions with each other create a pathway across dimensions through which she can consciously receive information from galactic and cosmic sources.

This pathway across dimensions is known as a rainbow bridge, or *antahkarana*. Much like the meridian systems organizing the functions of the human body, there are also pathways known as *ley lines* that follow fixed geometries across the body of the earth. And just as there are concentrations of energy running through your etheric body known as acupuncture points, *chakras* and *nadis*, so there are vortexes, portals and gateways within the etheric body of the earth.

Mother Earth, like you, also has a reproductive system, linked with akashic memories of stellar biology accessible to the whales. These memories are held within the magnetic fields which we spoke of earlier. During cycles of magnetic reversal, she is capable of giving birth to millions of new species within a surprisingly short period of time, even as other species go extinct. Morphogenetic fields for these new species can be drawn in from star systems and galaxies across the vast expanse of space, as well as from hidden dimensions beyond your own.

Would it help you if I personified her from now on, giving her a name that you can relate to? Shall I call her *Gaia*, so you can visualize and relate to her as the *Goddess* she is? I could also call her Aisha, given her new role as an embodiment of the *Earth Mother*, but I must admit that I am still too attached to perceiving her as my human teacher and friend!

Chapter 33

Earth Goddess

During the time Issa and his sons had been travelling in greater Britain, Aisha, Mirjan and I had become very close, and came to understand our individual tasks within this collective plan.

Aisha was to increasingly become the presence manifesting as *Mother Earth*. This may appear a bit far-fetched to some people, but do you know that the difference between a human and a planet is only a matter of scale, and that they are not so different as far a soul is concerned?

You are programmed to think that the body you inhabit is actually you, and therefore have a hard time imagining how a beautiful woman appearing in human form can actually hold the consciousness of a planet.

You will notice that within your human consciousness, all the actual functions of the body are performed by the body elemental. There is a hierarchy of elemental beings who maintain the life and health of the body, quite independent of the five *koshas*. Your mental consciousness is not required to understand the subtle intricacies of cellular functioning, and is more concerned with human needs such as communication, fulfilment, growth and knowledge. Your soul consciousness is linked with the *ahamkara*, or sense of self.

Your sense of self can expand far beyond the borders of the mind, and even the physical body. Aisha had taught us shamanic practices where we learned to experience ourselves as an entire universe. The experience of the soul is not limited to a single human expression, or a single human lifetime. Just as humans have higher bodies which enable them to subtle fields of light, *Mother Earth* also uses inter-dimensional portals to provide instantaneous access to worlds beyond your own.

So it is not a stretch of fantasy to imagine that Aisha had merged herself with the consciousness of our planet, allowing *Mother Earth* to experience within her evolutionary plan everything that Aisha herself had ever experienced or achieved.

What I am about to say now may sound a bit strange to some of you. But pay attention, because your next evolutionary step has to do with the mind rather than with physical bodies. You experience yourself as limited within the field of matter. You therefore imagine that the Fall had something to do with matter, and that matter is the densest expression of consciousness.

This is not true. The density is not within matter but within the mind. Your current root race was tasked with developing a state of mind capable of reason and logical thinking. You have succeeded in doing so, but in the process have significantly diminished your range of sense perceptions. Your sense of personal self has become identified with the personality structure rather than with the soul.

It is your perception of reality that creates your experience of reality. As your sense perceptions became limited, so did your ability to shape reality. Your mind became a reality reducing valve, forcing you into a continually diminishing consensus reality, where you began to identify the experience of density with your experience of matter.

But what if density was a product of mind, not matter? Consciousness pervades all things, and because matter is an extension of primordial consciousness, matter is imbued with all the powers of creation. The body is capable of being in all places at the same time, instantaneously moving through worlds and dimensions with the slightest intent.

The fact that you do not experience this has to do with illusions of the mind rather than with limitations within matter. The morphogenetic field associated with this illusionary state of mind is linked to the subtle geometrical structure known as the third dimensional grid system, which we have talked about. This grid system has been manipulated by a few key players to create a prison planet.

This is where my parents come in. It has been their responsibility to construct a *christ-consciousness grid* capable of transmuting the adverse effects of this raise matrix. In her previous manuscript my mother describes how Aisha succeeded in breaking through the third dimensional grid, and entering the womb of creation formerly known as the *underworld*, or *Hades*.

Consequently, this grid structure has begun to collapse, and is now being rapidly replaced by a higher dimensional grid capable of gestating a new root race responsive to the geometry of the soul. It has been my parents' task to ensure that this *christ-consciousness grid* is completed in time for the Great Shift.

Chapter 34

Collective Fields

What does it mean to establish a *christ-consciousness grid*? The guardians had asked my parents if they would be willing into the experience of human collective consciousness, and map this out within the grid systems of Gaia.

So while Issa was away with the boys in Britain, Mirjan had been working with Aisha to understand what this meant. She had come to recognize that each nation had its *folk soul,* which included not just humans but also elemental families associated with mountain ranges and river systems, landscapes and ecosystems.

The folk soul of India had been holding a position of spiritual leadership among the circle of nations. I suppose this is why so many of us are physically identified with this land. The Roman Empire represented political and economic leadership, a role that was passed on to Britain and various other countries in Europe once the Roman Empire had fallen.

The countries of the Middle East represent a historical bridge to the ancient past, while Latin America held dynamic new possibilities for emotional expression. Russia and China are stabilizing forces on the world stage while the New World was tasked with carrying the spirit of innovation. The USA is an uneasy contradiction of the native relationship with the land and the European need for ownership of land.

While Issa continued to travel across the world stabilizing the leylines, Mirjan's job was to enter the heart of each nation, and to bring the heart of humanity into a state of cohesion. This was to ensure that humanity would not extinguish itself in war and ecocide before they had the opportunity of going through the magnetic shift.

After Issa's return from Britain, the two of them learned to connect the leylines of the earth with inter-dimensional portals extending out to galactic fields associated with an incoming galactic superwave. This required bridging across dimensions to create a higher dimensional grid system which would eventually replace the current third dimensional magnetic grids hijacked by controlling forces to create a *saturnian matrix*.

In order to do this effectively, Aisha told them they would themselves need to take the rainbow body so they would have more access to subtle fields of human consciousness. It would be left to Chetan Nath to determine how best this could be accomplished.

In her first manuscript, Mirjan shared some teachings from Chetan Nath about taking the *rainbow body*. Here are two stages to this. The first, known as *kayakalpa*, is about extending life through a process of rejuvenation. The second is about creating a mind of light, which is capable of transforming the body into a body of light. In the Tibetan tradition this is known as the *rainbow body*. It is known in other traditions as the resurrected body, *diamond body, crystal body,* or *radiant body.*

Both of these stages involve changes within the DNA, and I will speak of this in more detail as we continue our journey together.

Chapter 35

Light of Hope

Building the higher dimensional grid system has to do with perceiving Gaia in her multi-dimensional wholeness, while at the same time experiencing yourself as a holographic unity.

The auric field surrounding your *koshas* goes through a significant shift once you learn to access the *anandamayakosha*. Once this access becomes permanent, you can transfer your identity very fluidly between personal, planetary, cosmic and universal aspects of being. You become an alchemist, with the power to enter the womb of creation, and give birth to infinite new possibilities.

As I hinted earlier, this was the task that my parents had been given. They were to penetrate the underworld of human experience, revealing the light of hope that continues to be held within the confused chaos of Pandora's box. In transforming chaos into creativity, despair to hope, darkness to light, their task was to change the subtle geometries within and around the planet in accordance with Gaia's evolutionary plan.

These grids can be mapped, and the geometries can be shaped. Ancient cultures around the world had mapped the *ley lines* and identified inter-dimensional portals at various crossings. Sometimes known as *power points,* these portals were used by dragon riders across the centuries to create new timelines.

It was these same grids that had been hijacked by dark magicians, however, to create a net of victimization and control extending into your own time, enslaving minds and bodies through acts of violence and greed, manipulating histories and narratives by promoting division, hatred and fear.

The good news is that the *saturnian matrix* will not survive the magnetic reversal which is soon to come. The bad news is that unless a higher vibrational matrix is able to replace the *saturnian matrix*, your planet will be plunged into a cataclysmic outcome much as what you experienced during the fall of Atlantis.

So perhaps you can better understand now the immensity of the task my parents were given. Their task was not to try and do this by themselves, but to inspire those who were ready to awaken the seeds of hope within their own being. Mirjan was given the job of presenting this archetypal story in words that could inspire future generations of alchemists, a task I am happy to continue on her behalf.

Meanwhile, in spite of all the distortions imposed by a corrupt priesthood, Issa's name had become well known around the world, and attracted many who were on the quest for their own holy grail. In their secluded lakeside ashram, Issa and Mirjan offered a way of integrating Vedic as well as Shamanic teachings, and continued to attract those with eyes to see, ears to hear, and hearts to understand their own roles within this cosmic story.

Chapter 36

Time Bubbles

What does it mean to replace the *saturnian matrix* with the *christ-consciousness grid*? Are there different geometries related to these? Will there be an instantaneous transition from one to the other during a magnetic reversal? What can we expect to happen on the other side of this event?

These are important questions, and the answer has to do with the fundamental nature of time and space.

Each dimension of reality operates according to its own laws of physics, which includes our experience of time and space. When you leave the physical body at death, your astral and causal bodies experience time very differently. You will remember also how time moves very differently in the otherworld of the *sidhe*, or within the inner earth, or dimensions inhabited by fairy and angelic kingdoms.

The magnetic reversal is a unique moment where two dimensions begin to intersect, which means that two very different versions of time begin to confront each other. You will remember that Hiranya and Arwyn could easily observe humans wandering around in third dimensional reality, but ordinary humans were not able to see them or sense their presence unless they knew how to stretch their etheric senses, or were deliberately invited to join them.

You could say that these two worlds operate in different dimensional realities. *Time bubbles* are different from *timelines*. While timelines have to do with future probabilities, time bubbles show up when you are shifting from one dimension of reality into another.

A good analogy would be the birth of a child. Within the matrix of the womb, the child experiences itself in a relatively limited physical environment, while being highly attuned to the astral worlds. Once it is born, a brand-new physical environment opens up while the astral worlds fall away. But as it goes through the birth tunnel, a time bubble is created which contains both worlds, so that the transition from one world to another can be accomplished smoothly.

The tunnel of birth represents a time when the physical and astral worlds come together, allowing the soul to incarnate, even if only to a limited extent. The same thing can be said of the magnetic reversal. A tunnel opens between the worlds so that the soul can be released from the stickiness of the *saturnian matrix*, and incarnate again more fully. The difference is that whereas birth is a personal event, the magnetic reversal is a planetary event.

As the magnetic field collapses, time and eternity merge, while space and infinity also experience a meeting point. This provides an opportunity for new worlds to be created, new species to be born, and new evolutionary pathways to unfold in the twinkling of an eye. A new dimensional reality can be collectively manifested, as long as proper preparations have been made.

Evolution has a tendency to proceed gradually over many thousands of years, followed by a quantum leap during these times of magnetic reversal. What happens when the magnetic fields begin to strengthen after the collapse and reversal? Quantum leaps are an opportunity for a higher dimensional timeline to replace an existing timeline, provided that the planetary grids can support this.

What most people are likely to experience during the magnetic reversal is the sense of waking up from a dream. You would wake up from a dull grey reality with an extremely limited range of sense perceptions into a luminous world of multi-dimensional awareness. The same thing happens when the soul leaves the physical body at death. Doorways to astral worlds are opened, and realms of magic and wonder suddenly appear.

The template for this new earth consciousness already exists as an overlay within your current experience of reality. But now comes the moment of choice. Many of you are finding yourselves being increasingly pulled apart within yourselves, as if you were standing with one foot upon the shore, and the other foot on a sailboat moving rapidly out towards the wide ocean.

Some of you may be experiencing a period of time where nothing seems to make sense anymore. The old ways are dying but the new has not yet been born. Like a caterpillar within its cocoon, you find yourself in a transitional state with no familiar guideposts. You feel achingly alone, the trappings of a safe and familiar world dissolve, and you find yourself wondering whether anything you have accomplished is meaningful anymore.

This state of consciousness is sometimes referred to as the *dark night of the soul.* When you find yourself going through these moments, do not resist, for it is part of an alchemical process where cherished illusions of a personal self are falling away. Like contractions preceding the moment of birth, the frequency and intensity of these dark nights will continue to increase as you approach the magnetic reversal. The more empty you allow yourself to become, the more light you will embody in your moment of rebirth.

Many prophecies refer to *three days of darkness* as a prelude to the moment of collective birth. Given the shifts you have already made in recent years, you will assuredly pass through as a species, but the journey will be easier if you provide yourself a map for where you are going, especially if you can hold the memory of who you essentially are!

Chapter 37

Mind of Light

Forgive me, I keep making these time jumps where I start off describing events in a specific period of time, then end up in a completely different time zone. But perhaps you will get used to this, for this story transcends linear time, and is layered through multiple eras and dimensions of reality.

So let us leapfrog back now to the time of Issa and Mirjan. We were talking about their journey through the underworlds, their work with the *christ-consciousness grids*, and with seeding new possibilities into the morphogenetic fields of *Gaia*.

This work required an ability to penetrate the mysteries of separation while being simultaneously anchored in a state of unity. It required an ability to witness the veiling power of the *kanchukas* while not being bound by them. It required that they could access primordial consciousness in the midst of ordinary life, in order to anchor this awareness into the grid systems of the Earth.

As they continued to work with their circle of disciples, Aisha showed up one day, calmly announcing that it was time for them now to take the rainbow body. Just like herself, the two of them were being asked by *Gaia* to move on to a different level of work within immortalized physical bodies for the next cycle of ages.

There is not a single path to taking the *rainbow body*. Chetan Nath achieved this in the way of his Nath tradition, long and arduous, with single minded purpose and lengthy initiations. Aisha achieved this through her deep understanding of the *tattwas*, and then making her journey into the underworld. Hiranya accomplished the first stage of this process through his sensitivity to the natural world, and his connections with the *sidhe*.

Common to each of these was the unwavering commitment to being in service to the *Great Mother*. This requires emptiness and surrender, as Aisha has spoken about so eloquently in a previous manuscript. Your current root race is not yet qualified to take this path, because there are too many splits within the ego, too much attachment to the personal self, too much absorption with the requirements of the human story.

Once you recognize that being human is only a small part of who you are, however, the journey can begin. Aisha often speaks about the three stages of enlightenment. In the first stage you are no longer unconscious, but have identified as a seeker, as a human entity, a drop of water moving through the rivers of life towards the sea.

In the second stage, you enter the great ocean, and you dissolve. There is no more separation, no more identification with the personal story, no more seeking, even for enlightenment. You become empty of everything except the desire to serve the greater wholeness. You remain human but are no longer identified with your humanness.

And then comes the third stage. Here the ocean enters the drop, and moves through the human vessel according to its own plan and purpose. Anything remaining of a fixed story is obliterated in a blast of primordial sound. Any attachments to a personal self are swept away in a great cosmic wind. The limiting effect of the five *kanchukas*, described so eloquently by Aisha in a previous manuscript, are shattered.

The morphogenetic field within the DNA becomes receptive to the pulse of planetary, galactic and universal forces. The mind moves across multiple dimensions into archetypal realms, creating a *mind of light* capable of receiving the pulse of the *Great Mother*. And then finally, in a flash of radiance, the physical body dies, only to be simultaneously reborn.

In this rebirth of physical consciousness, you are no longer subject to a *saturnian matrix* which perceives physical existence through the limiting influence of the *kanchukas*. The veil of *maya* is pierced and the fullness of *Self* incarnates into the *mind of light*. A primordial ocean of infinite consciousness pours into holographic receptors within your DNA, creating a *body of light*.

This will be your destiny in root races to come. This is the template I have been tasked with creating and building. I will be sharing more of my own story later in this manuscript. But first, let us continue with my parents, Issa and Mirjan.

Chapter 38

Body of Light

Issa and Mirjan had grown towards a ripe old age. They had served their little kingdom of Kash for many years. Their band of disciples had grown, and many had been taught in the ways of truth and light.

Hiranya and Eliyakim had followed their destinies in Greater Britain, where they remained for the rest of their lives. I missed their physical companionship, but we were never really apart, for we had built inner bridges of communication, and continued to follow each other wherever we chose to be.

Aisha recognized that Issa and Mirjan were ready now to take the rainbow body, and move into the next phase of their service. And so the time came, after a period of preparation with Chetan Nath and then with Aisha, when they slipped away into the valley of Nubra, several days east in the region of Ladakh, where they remained together for a moon, deep in motionless samadhi, completing the final stages of their ascension.

A great luminosity accompanied them on their return. Like Aisha, they could now slip in and out of dimensions as needed, and even across time. While Mirjan remained for a while to take care of their kingdom, Issa disappeared with a few disciples into the high peaks of the Himalayas, towards the source of the Ganga. It was said of him later that his chariot streaked across the skies as he departed to the home of Shiva.

Mirjan and I stayed together within our palace home in Srinagar for a couple years, long enough so she could hand the reins of our little kingdom over to me, and for her to finish writing her two manuscripts, *Issa Son of the Sun* and *Mirjan Daughter of the Moon*.

It was a precious time for the two of us, as we shared intimate memories of her childhood, her meetings with Issa, and the years that followed. Afterwards, we decided where it was necessary to hide these manuscripts, so they could be found by the right people at the right time as inspiration for an awakening world.

We continued to have inter-dimensional adventures together, visited occasionally by Aisha. I found myself rapidly entering a body of light during this time. As I have said before, I had been given the gift to absorb new possibilities directly into my cellular consciousness, and just being around Aisha and my parents all these years was all it took to create my own rainbow body.

Rulership was dynastic in those days, so in the absence of my brothers, I had agreed to take on this responsibility for a while. Then one day, as Aisha, Mirjan and I met together one last time in Aisha's cave by the river, my beautiful mother vanished in a burst of light to go join Issa and their band of disciples. There were no goodbyes necessary, since there was no more separation between us, and we would always remain within each other in the continuation of our shared journey.

PART II

SOUL OF THE UNIVERSE

Chapter 39

Transitions

And now, with some of these loose ends tied together, it is time to move more fully into my own story. Those of you who have read my mother's manuscript already know that my DNA was rather permeable to thoughts and intentions, that I only needed to see something or experience something a few times in order to admit this into my cellular consciousness.

And once I had experienced something in my physical consciousness, this gift then became available to be seeded into the collective consciousness of an emerging humanity, for my role as a *manu* was indeed to become the template for a new root race.

Taking the rainbow body was therefore not the end of my journey, but the beginning. This task had been quickly accomplished during the time my mother and I spent together writing, or dictating to me, her two manuscripts. When not busy with these manuscripts, or teaching me about running our small kingdom, we would find ourselves happily travelling across timelines and dimensions, disappearing and reappearing as Aisha had taught us to do.

This was a time of gathering gifts to be planted in the collective consciousness of a new humanity, received from a multitude of star systems across galaxies physical as well as non-physical. I would weave them together into a new matrix of possibility, and then plant them into the *christ-consciousness grid* which my parents had already begun to build.

After Mirjan left to rejoin Issa and their small band of disciples, I continued this task, often with the help and support of Aisha. The time came when my nephew Elan, second son of Eliyakim and Sara, consented to join me in the valley of Kash in order to apprentice with me and eventually take over the kingdom I had been entrusted with.

He married eventually, and his own lineage continued through the generations. I need not go into the details of this story, except to say that his genealogy going back to Issa can still be found in modern day Kashmir, inscribed in the annals of time through record keepers such as Bashir el Kamini.

Names and stories have changed, as tends to happen when a succession of invading cultures create new stories from the shadows of history. But a tomb still exists in Srinagar containing relics such as nails and hair attributed to my father, Issa, as he completed his ascension into the rainbow body.

Chapter 40

Multi-Dimensionality

Reality is a multi-dimensional ladder, with multiple levels of mind linked to infinite realms of existence, each connected to different dimensions of space and time. Our shamans taught that there are vertical doorways that lead into 'upper' worlds of spirit and 'lower' worlds of nature. There are also doorways that are 'holographic' in nature, where the experience of reality has nothing to do with concepts of size, time or distance.

Most of you have become fixated with a single dimension within the complexity of time and space, which measures everything in terms of physical size and distance, or linear time and causality. The key to understanding ourselves, the Earth, and the Universe, however, is to recognize that the universe is a hologram, and that each part of this hologram extends into infinity above as well as infinity below. Every atom contains a universe. And the entire universe is but a single Consciousness, which is who we are.

When I speak about the upper worlds of spirit and the lower worlds of nature, I am not referring to a hierarchy of worlds. I am not even saying that these worlds are separate from each other. They are all linked through electrical and magnetic fields which pervade the universe and which we experience as the holographic consciousness of *Gaia*.

When we are identified exclusively with the human form, our consciousness remains limited to third dimensional perceptions of time and space. Once these doorways open, however, we begin to touch the Soul of the Earth, and the Soul of the Universe. We understand the meaning of Indra's Net, and learn that we are not only learning to perceive reality in a different way but also directly influencing reality in each moment of existence.

We enter the evolutionary stream of *Gaia*, moving towards an evolutionary potential that has remained dormant within our human biology. We understand that our purpose for existence as humans is to enter the consciousness of *Gaia* and to shape this evolution. We are here to slip behind causal interpretations of reality, and enter a holographic dimension where everything in this vast universe becomes functionally connected. Each cell opens up to an entire planet. And each star becomes a luminous cell within a galactic self.

Given this holographic understanding of the universe, let us take another look at *Gaia's* multi-dimensional consciousness, and how each of us might begin to experience this directly. We have learned to experience the Earth through a 'middle world' fixation of size and distance being perceived as real outside of ourselves.

Once the upper, middle and lower worlds become unified within our consciousness, however, we begin to experience the Soul of *Gaia*, which in turn is holographically linked with the Soul of the Sun, the Galaxy, and infinite realms beyond. We understand that this infinite interconnected Soul is who we are! Or as Aisha is fond of reminding us, "That I AM"!

We cannot relate to the soul of the Earth as long as we perceive ourselves as located within time and space. But once we loosen our field of perception, and discover that time and space are instead located within us, then we enter a holographic dimension where we enter into communication with all beings as a holographic extension of our own being, and discover that there is a single field of intelligence and presence at the heart of it all.

Just as humans are designed to experience ourselves as interpenetrating fields of awareness linked together through the geomagnetic fields of the earth, so is *Gaia* linked to energetic forces of creation extending out past our Sun and solar system, out through the Central Sun of our own galaxy, out through infinite fields of plasma that comprise the totality of Indra's Net.

Chapter 41

Evolutionary Plan

There are species of life on your planet, such as the whales, who are capable of accessing the field of cosmic unity. Humans had this capacity during earlier ages, and you experience this still as a longing for oneness. It is your destiny during future root races to recover this capacity, entering a field of memory where new cycles of creation can be shaped, by accessing levels of universal intelligence holographically linked to your DNA.

I wish to emphasize again that just as humans are essentially comprised of a skeletal system, a circulatory system, a respiratory system, a nervous system, a lymphatic system, an immune system, and so on, so is the Earth a single living entity comprised of interactive systems.

As I have said before, rocks and minerals comprise her skeletal system, clouds, rivers and oceans comprise her circulatory system, trees and forests her respiratory system. Animals represent different aspects of her sensory, emotional and nervous systems. Whales, humans and most animals are capable of self-reflection, looking within the mirror of creation to discover themselves as an integral part of this web of life.

Just as humans are comprised of a set of interconnected bodies, so is *Gaia*. As we learn to interact with subtle, astral and causal aspects of our human existence, we simultaneously come into relationship with the subtle, astral and causal bodies of our beautiful living planet.

We learn that time functions differently as we begin accessing the higher bodies of the Earth. We learn that space, size and distance are no longer what we currently imagine. We learn that the boundary between 'inside' and 'outside' becomes very permeable. We learn that we are holographically linked to the multi-dimensional totality of *Gaia*, and to the *Great Mother* incarnating as an entire Universe.

From a purely third-dimensional perspective, humans have become a cancer on the face of the Earth, close to destroying our host planet and its intricate balance of life through our thoughtlessness, arrogance and greed. From a multi-dimensional perspective, however, we are a species in transition, still growing in maturity, still learning to take our proper place in the evolutionary stream of *Gaia*.

Our purpose lies not in the accomplishments of the past but in what we are yet to achieve. *Gaia* as a highly evolved soul is capable of nurturing us with unconditional love until we fulfil the purpose we were created for, which is to become a bridge across multiple dimensions of reality as the nervous system of the Earth.

How is this accomplished? The evolutionary plan of *Gaia* is bigger than our ability to distort or sabotage this process. From a multi-dimensional perspective there is nothing which can ultimately go wrong about this world or about ourselves. Our mistakes are evolutionary gateways. Every crisis becomes an opportunity for new pathways to emerge. Diamonds are simply chunks of coal hardened under pressure. As we evolve towards the next species of humanity, Homo Luminous, the purpose of our current experience of separation and duality is revealed and transcended.

What then is *Gaia's* evolutionary plan? *Gaia* to me is a multidimensional consciousness. She herself is linked through etheric doorways to the sun, to the galaxy, to the entire cosmos and to the Spirit that moves through all things. If I am a multi-dimensional being capable of experiencing myself as the One Self that moves through all things, so it is with *Gaia*. I can express myself within her as she experiences herself within me. As above so below, as within so without. We are each a pearl within Indra's Net.

Chapter 42

Plasma Cosmology

Forgive me if I delve into a little bit of science here. There is a higher dimensional perception of the cosmos that your scientists are finally beginning to understand, which is being called the *Electric Universe Theory*, or *Plasma Cosmology*. It postulates that everything in the universe is connected with everything else through filaments of electrical force, or *plasma*, which is an ionized state of matter that comprises 99.9% percent of the physical universe.

Most of what you recognize as matter across the universe began as *plasma*. Plasma is created through the action of electrical fields operating within the *tattwas,* which Aisha has described much more fully in *Daughter of the Moon*. The interaction between electrical fields and magnetic fields across various dimensions of time and space create states of matter ranging from causal to astral, and ultimately the physical realms where you currently find your home.

What you call the periodic table of elements is found within every dimension of creation. But it is the proportion between plasma and physical substance that determines which dimension you find yourself within. Once you fully understand this, you will recognize that the fabric of time and space is structured differently than you imagine, and that your current understanding of quantum physics is still very much incomplete.

Primal electrical fields shape consciousness, shape physical reality, shape the formation of galaxies and solar systems, planets and life. When electrical fields condense from plasma into physical matter, and then towards the formation of life within these fields of matter, magnetic fields are generated in order to sustain this state of reality.

Some of your scientists have talked about *dark energy* or *dark matter,* as attempts to reconcile this 99.9% of the universe which cannot be measured in physical terms. They forget however that physical matter is only the tip of the iceberg, and that magnetism is not simply a force of attraction, but a field of memory and divine intention spanning many dimensions.

There are multi-dimensional doorways operating within subtle electrical and magnetic fields that permeate all existence. Electrical forces help us connect with the upper worlds, expanding out into the Universe, while magnetic fields connect us with the lower worlds, our connection with nature and the Earth. As we learn to simultaneously open doorways to the upper as well as lower worlds, we find ourselves expanding out into the universe while also remaining firmly grounded upon the Earth.

Your emerging understanding of *Plasma Cosmology* is very similar to the metaphor of *Indra's Net.* If we extend our understanding of this model, since everything is simultaneously linked with everything else, you understand that time does not exist in a literal sense. What happens in one moment of time leaves an imprint across all moments of existence. What you experience as a single physical lifetime bridges across to all lifetimes ever experienced, past and future.

The same goes for space. As long as you perceive space as something outside of you, you will measure things in terms of distances, whether it's miles or light years. But when you experience that space exists inside you, rather than the other way around, an enormous paradigm shift takes place. What happens in one corner of the universe is instantaneously transmitted and perceived everywhere else. You enter into a holographic experience of the universe, and start experiencing yourself as infinite creative Consciousness.

Once the doorways of perception begin to open, you will learn to access levels of mind beyond the rational mind, such as the higher mind, the illumined mind, the intuitive mind, the overmind and the supermind, each of which takes you into progressive states of expanded identity.

Your experience of reality, as well as your ability to shape reality, is very different within each of these levels of mind. Very few of you have gained the ability to access these higher levels of mind. In times to come, this will become commonplace, however, as you move into a cycle of conscious evolution.

Chapter 43

Cosmic Seeding

Our shamanic traditions recognize that the entire universe is an incarnation of the *Great Mother* and a reflection of the *Great Mother*. *Gaia* herself is a reflection and incarnation of the *Her*, just as we are. Once we understand this, we begin to enter into a relationship with *Gaia* where we become midwives for a new creation.

As long as you remain in ignorance of this truth, you will remain trapped in a paradigm which will inevitably lead your species towards extinction. But once you understand the holographic nature of the universe, you will enter into cellular dimensions of mind capable of creating new evolutionary pathways, including a new biological species of humanity.

From a multidimensional perspective, this has already happened within the subtle bodies of the Earth. Now we need to bring that subtle blueprint into physical form and structure. Your destiny as an evolving human species is to consciously participate in this evolution. To the extent you can dissociate from linear time, this process can happen very quickly, and perhaps even instantaneously.

Many of you are coming to understand that you live multiple incarnations, that the human personality is only one tiny aspect of the journey that you have been travelling as a soul. However, you still think of these incarnations as a linear sequence, forgetting that the soul does not operate in linear time, and can therefore take on multiple incarnations simultaneously.

So with the background I have provided, you will understand now when I tell you that my greater oversoul has taken many incarnations on this earth at various historical times, and that these memories and experiences span many thousands of years. The body I currently wear is an immortal body, but the oversoul can still incarnate in seemingly separate personalities across the illusion of time.

The incarnations I have experienced are not just human. Before I ever came to this Earth I travelled through planetary systems in stars and galaxies beyond your own. You could say I was extra-terrestrial then, just as most of you have also been. But I have taken incarnation within other species upon this planet as well, within the dwellers beneath the surface of the earth who call themselves *Agarthan*, within some of the former root races of humanity, such as *Angels, Hyperboreans, Lemurians* and *Atlanteans,* and also within non-human species who are just as necessary to *Gaia's* evolutionary journey as your own race of humans.

With the help of Aisha and the Guardians, I have woven the memories of these incarnations into the higher dimensional grid systems of the Earth, and into the template of a new humanity. Your human genetics contained much of this information in earlier times, but your current root race has become warped from falling into the density of duality, and has lost some of the codes for multidimensional access. You have therefore trapped yourselves in a prison of your own making, and you have thrown away the keys.

It is time to find these keys again as you step towards the sixth root race, *Homo Luminous*.

Chapter 44

Shambala

I will share some words now about the Guardians of the Earth, and the role they have played in shaping *Gaia's* evolutionary destiny. These Guardians include those you call *ascended masters*, many of whom have taken the rainbow body in earlier cycles of human history. Ancient *saptarishis, manus* from earlier ages, extra-terrestrial masters, elven and elemental teachers, forest guides, and more recently, some of the *nath* lineage, have also joined this select group. Some of them are distinctly non-human, as I will say more about later.

While the majority of them maintain physical bodies, they are for the most part multidimensional, and can move in and out of physical density. Some of them exist within etheric or astral bodies, but are also capable of taking on physical density when needed. They each bring their own skills and abilities, and have in common their total dedication to serving *Gaia* in her evolutionary journey.

There are councils that take place at certain times of the year as needed, where many of them will come together to open portals, share information, or prepare for cycles ahead. More rarely, they will come together when there are emergency situations that threaten the survival of a species or the planet.

They meet in various places across the earth, sometimes in caverns beneath the earth, sometimes at power centers or galactic portals, sometimes even within the causal planes in cities such as *Shambala*, also known as the *Halls of Amenti.*

There it was that Aisha took me one day, soon after my mother Mirjan had departed to join Issa and their disciples in the lower Himalayan ranges alongside the Ganga. We arrived in Shambala like we usually travelled, teleporting across dimensions. For most adepts, teleporting through physical dimensions is, as you call it, *a piece of cake.* It does take a bit more practice to move through higher astral and causal worlds while retaining physical bodies, but with Aisha to guide me, we accomplished this just as easily.

I was surprised to see how many of the Guardians had gathered together on this occasion. I was happy to meet Aranyani and we spent some time together as she gave me an update on Hiranya and Arwyn. It was also good to see Chetan Nath, who had been an illustrious teacher for both my parents, and I also spent time with the *manus* of earlier root races learning from them about weaving genetic material from across star systems into an existing human species.

It turned out that this particular gathering was held mostly as a support for me. As the *manu* of the sixth and seventh root races, a role I had happily accepted many years ago, my bodies would need to be fine-tuned with appropriate codes and frequencies. I was told I would also need to be placed into a state of *incubation,* or what the ancient ones called *suspended animation,* for a period of time, so that I could enter more deeply into the mind of *Gaia.*

Shambala exists within the inmost regions of the Earth, lit by the luminosity of a self-existing light. Built from pillars of white marble stretching to the sky, it is an architectural prototype for some of the most beautiful cities every built. It may surprise some people to imagine that there is any form of life beneath the surface of the earth, but I can tell you that nothing on the surface of your planet currently compares to the splendor of the inner earth, and the network of cities within causal, astral as well as etheric planes known collectively as *Agartha*.

Do you know that life exists in every dimension of existence? There are planets that look dead to you physically but are teeming with life in etheric and astral dimensions. The same is true inside the earth. Some cities are close to the surface, and exist on a dimensional frequency close to your own. Many voyagers have unwittingly made their way there, whether going in through polar gateways or while exploring cave systems leading down from the surface.

As you go deeper down into the Earth's center you discover astral cities of differing density, often connected together through transport systems similar to your own, but faster and perhaps a bit more elegant. Shambala exists within the causal planes, and could therefore be considered a heavenly city. Here, within the most sacred of temples, had come together the Council of Guardians.

Chapter 45

Choice Point

We sat within an amphitheater, 12 pillars around the circumference stretching up to a domed ceiling. Geometrical symbols of power and crystals of every color imaginable created a ring of presence around us. An open sarcophagus made of polished granite was placed upon a raised dais in front of the amphitheater. Twelve of the elders sat in a half circle around this, with the rest of the group linked together in widening circles around, all facing inwards.

I was invited to sit in front of the sarcophagus, face to face with Aisha. A great and solemn hush fell upon the entire assembly as together we waited for the proceedings to open.

Thoth, as Manu for the current race of humanity, was the first to speak. He is also known as Hermes Trismegistus by the Greeks, who knew him as a messenger between humanity and the elder gods.

"Ten thousand years have passed since the vibrational densities on this planet shifted," he began. "Atlantis had fallen, and great technological marvels were lost beneath the sea, along with a race who had learned for a time to wield the power of the gods. They had not learned however, to temper this power with wisdom. Creation cannot be held in balance when hearts have been corrupted with arrogance. The greatest achievements count for nothing when the circle of life has been broken.

"And so it was that a new root race came into being, whose task was to learn about balance. Their powers had been intentionally curtailed until they would be deemed wise enough to handle the mighty powers of creation. I was given the responsibility for shepherding this race. I regret to say I was not very successful, and half a cycle later, with the Great Flood of Nuh, was forced to begin again.

"The time has come when the human race is once again at a choice point. Two thousand years still remain until the completion of this cycle, but already there are indications that this experiment too will end in failure, this time perhaps with the extinction of the Earth itself.

"This cannot be allowed. This gathering has been convened in order to find a solution to this crisis, at a time that is pivotal not only in the evolution of this planet but also within the current cycle of galactic and universal history."

"Each of you within this circle are key players in this evolutionary drama," he continued, "but I fear your efforts will not be enough. Each of you invited here to this Council has achieved a balance between love, wisdom and power, but there are too few of us here to make a significant impact upon a race lost in delusion and destined for self-destruction.

"I come before you therefore with a heart sick with grief, for like many of you here I have seen the future, and seen an extinction level event coming that could be more cataclysmic even than the Fall of Atlantis."

He turned then towards my beloved teacher Aisha. "Aisha here has penetrated the depths of the human underworld," he stated. "She understands the challenges we will face, that humanity will face. If anyone here can provide a path of return, it is she. She has been given charge of our precious daughter Elmira, whom we have called together from realms of future starlight. What have you to tell us now, dear sister?"

Aisha took my hands within her own, and gazed into my eyes for a deep moment. She sighed then, and addressed the assembly. "Our beloved Elmira sits before us all now, a worthy successor to Mirjan, Daughter of the Moon, who was my beloved student and companion before her, and to Issa, Son of the Sun, most magnificent of men. She holds within her a potential almost completely veiled from the lost heart of humanity, all that is best and most beautiful, all that could emerge in collective biology when the time is right."

She looked slowly around the circle, holding each one gathered within her gaze. "I implore you to not judge this troublesome race through the shifting eyes of circumstances, but through the eyes of a vision still unbroken. We have seen the effects of Pandora's Box, which was opened before humanity was ready to handle these inner forces. The effects of this you see all around you, and it grieves me too. But I also have seen the secret hope that remains within the box. I have seen that man's finest hour comes often in times of greatest peril, his greatest strength in times of extreme weakness."

She turned then towards Thoth, and sighed again, "You are right, my brother. Even she, with all the gifts she has been given, is not strong enough to overturn the trajectory that humanity has set upon. But we can give our strength to her, infuse her soul with the power that flows through each of us. I can support her with the power of the *Earth Mother* that moves through me now, and perhaps together we can create a timeline wherein a new earth consciousness can be birthed."

Chapter 46

Underworld Journey

There were nods of assent around the circle, and more than one set of eyes moist with tenderness and tears. It was decided I needed to revisit the underworld, enter the collective darkness of humanity as Aisha had once done, and set free the power of hope within the deep recesses of Pandora's Box. Only thus could I weave together the forgotten powers of creation and discover the required alchemy to heal the lost heart of humanity.

It would be a dangerous descent, just as Aisha had once made when my mother was still young, opening up a first ray of hope on behalf of humanity. I knew that this time the task would be even more arduous, for I was being asked to intercede on behalf of a race lost in the fog, completely divorced from the guiding light of its own collective soul.

A premonition of dread weighted heavy on my heart. What are the chances I would succeed when even Thoth had given up? I missed seeing my parents in this circle. They should have been here, but I was told that the decision I needed to make was mine alone to make, and they did not want to unduly influence me one way or the other. Would seeing them here have interfered with what needed to be done?

Yes, I was close to a hundred and twenty years of age now, but I too needed to grow into my calling, entering my own flow of sovereignty. In any case, I felt their presence strong within me, and felt their concern as well as their pride in this step I had chosen to take.

Aisha took me by the hand and helped me inside the sarcophagus. She looked deeply into my eyes. "Go, my beautiful daughter, I will be with you no matter where you are. You will not be alone." Her eyes grew moist with tears as she stroked my face and laid me inside. She had made this journey before, and knew how difficult and dangerous it could be. My mother Mirjan had been her protector then; she would be mine now.

A heavy granite lid was placed over the top so there was complete darkness and isolation inside. The sarcophagus had been built so it was energetically aligned with significant portals within the earth and across the galaxy, and was designed to provide protection for my physical body as I travelled out wherever I needed to go.

One by one, the Guardians came, sat in front of the sarcophagus, and gave their blessing, then continued their vigil in the sacred circle. Each of them was reaching into a deep inner source of light, which they were radiating out to me. I could feel their presence in the darkness of the sarcophagus as I slowly descended into the underworld.

It wasn't long before I found myself crossing the river Styx, dividing the worlds of the living and the dead. Some of you today may have had near death experiences where you found yourself entering into realms of incredible beauty and light. It wasn't always so, however. In the depths of *kali yuga*, the collective soul of humanity had become chained to a reincarnation cycle where they had become completely cut off from the light of the soul, even between incarnations. Aisha's own descent into the underworld all those decades ago helped release the first seeds of hope. But there was much more work to be done.

Suddenly a dark presence took form in front of me. It was Anubis, also known as Yama or Hades, holding out his famous scales, where the heart of a departed soul would be weighed against a feather, to see if it was worthy to be raised into light. It was a stern test. How many of us even in this august circle could ever consider ourselves worthy? And now here was Anubis with me, wishing to weigh, not a single heart alone, but the collective heart of humanity.

"Stop my child. Do not enter further. Give up your foolish quest on behalf of humanity, or you will surely find yourself lost in these realms forever."

Anubis was an imposing presence, and I felt sincerity and truth in his statement. I too could be stubborn however. "I cannot turn my back now upon humanity, my Lord Anubis. You know I come to plead not only on behalf of a race that exists today but also a race that is still to come. I ask to be tested within these scales on humanity's behalf."

"So be it," sighed Anubis. "I did not expect any less from you, for you are more than worthy of your lineage with Issa and Mirjan. But consider yourself warned Elmira. What you behold now will not be easy, even for you."

Chapter 47

The Choice

Slowly then, with increasing rapidity, a series of images flashed before my eyes. There were tribes and nations warring on each other in a frenzy of rape, pillage and plunder. Blood-stained warriors mad with lust laughed hysterically as they raped every woman they could find, forcing them to watch as they swung their babies around in circles until their brains bashed open against walls of rock. New systems of torture were devised across the millennia, seemingly without end. Those who resisted, spoke out, or offered healing were hunted down, mutilated and burned.

With the growth of technology came ever new ways of waging war and terror, each more horrible than before. Gunpowder and mortars were used to blast each other to smithereens. Napalm, cluster bombs, toxic chemicals and nerve gases were used on enemy combatants who went screaming in agony to their graves. Ultimately came the atom bomb and the hydrogen bomb, weapons of mass destruction that threatened not only the survival of one planet, but multiple dimensions of life linked with physical matter through nuclear chains.

Meanwhile, entire species of animals were being exterminated for their skins or for their horns. Whales were being hunted down in their thousands for their blubber. Sharks were being exterminated in the millions simply for their fins, and then left to die horrible deaths as they were thrown back alive into the sea. Big game hunters engaged in canned hunting, where frightened lions and antelopes darted around in an enclosed space where there was no escape. Animals designated to be consumed for food were penned up their entire lives in filthy corrals only to be brutally slaughtered for the dinner table.

Rivers and oceans had become toxic with chemicals and plastic wastes. The atmosphere had turned poisonous and cancerous. Grains and vegetables no longer had the power to nourish, but were rapidly depleting the soil. The cycle of life had been broken. Millions of species of precious life had vanished forever from the face of the earth.

Technologies using discordant frequencies wreaked havoc with the nervous systems of humans and mammals. Blood sacrifices using satanic rituals fed a soulless elite hungry for power. Man no longer had the ability to touch their souls. Divided among themselves, ruled by a banking elite that existed only for their own lust for power, an entire population of humans had allowed themselves to become slave masters and predators, or else oppressed sheep fearfully led to their own slaughter.

As I lived and felt these rapidly growing series of images, spanning endless centuries past and future, my entire being groaned in agonizing pain. I felt shattered and broken beyond redemption. Aisha's promise of presence and support remained only a faint memory. I could no longer feel her, or the Guardians, or even my own parents.

Most terrifying of all, I could no longer feel the presence of the *Great Mother* within me or around me. Like never before in all my long years of existence, I felt hopelessly and irretrievably lost. As my heart became increasingly burdened by the weight of humanity's darkness, I felt how it was no longer able to sustain the lightness of the feather on the other side of Anubis' scales. Like arm wrestling against a superior opponent, however fiercely and stubbornly I continued to fight, I could feel my strength failing.

The voice of Anubis boomed within me continuing to speak his ugly truth, "Why should humanity be saved, *Child of the Stars*? What makes them worthy to dwell upon this beautiful earth? Why should I not exterminate them now like the vermin they have become?"

I did not have an answer for Anubis. "No, no, this cannot be, my heart kept imploring as it slowly began to sink ever deeper into despair. Take this vision away from me," my soul sobbed in agony. I had never allowed myself to feel before this darkness of the human spirit. "They are more than this, I kept repeating in my dazed stupor. This is not real, it is just the shell, just the illusion, we are so much more than this, so much more."

The dark visions kept coming however. How could the new root race be birthed if this current race was to be obliterated, I kept asking myself? Anubis then reminded me of Sekhmet, the beautiful lion headed goddess, who had been tasked by the gods to destroy humanity during an earlier cycle. She too had resisted at first, but then she had been shown the future of a planet empty and desolate, all life destroyed in toxic fumes and nuclear conflagration.

This vision finally touched her lion heart. Roaring in rage as well as deep sadness for what she was being asked to do, she went on a rampage, berserk with the pain of what she was being shown, obliterating the last traces of humans upon the earth, save for two.

"You are being given this same power now, Elmira. Choose for yourself a man from among this wretched race of humans. Your task is not to rescue these broken and unworthy creatures, but to create a race worthy of *Gaia*, worthy of the great potential she has nurtured and harbored within her."

Chapter 48

The Whales

"I cannot do this," I persisted. *Gaia* is also the face of the *Great Mother*. Can a mother sacrifice any of her children, even if for the sake of the many? I cannot do this. There must be another way."

"There is no other way," Anubis' voice continued to boom within me. "This is your task now, Elmira, whether you wish this or not. Will you hold yourself responsible for another great catastrophe spawned by this errant race? Will you wait until it is once again too late? You have been invited by the *Earth Mother* to join your heart with hers. You must help her now in her time of dire need."

"As representative for humanity I give you the power to accomplish this task now. All you must do is to allow the scales with the collective human heart to sink to the bottom, and I will take care of this in my own way. Do not fail the *Mother* now."

Even in the depths of my despair I heard the voice of my own beating heart. "This is NOT the way of the *Mother*," I screamed into the gathering darkness. "The *Mother* is patient. She has waited entire cycles for this race to awaken. Humanity is still in its infancy. They deserve another chance. They will fulfil the task they have been given. I know this. I will move earth and heaven itself to accomplish this."

I could feel my strength returning now. "I do not know how humanity will be redeemed, nor do I know if the Earth will be destroyed. But I DO know the heart of the *Mother*, and this is not the way." I spoke with certainty now. "Forgive me, my Lord Anubis. But I know what must be done now. I will NOT allow this to happen."

And then I heard the songs of the whales, singing to me from far away. They sang of a time of maturity and forgiveness. They spoke from a collective wisdom, from memories held in the oceans, from memories belonging to an ancient future.

"We too have suffered at the hands of humans," I heard their voices inside me. "But it is the way of the *Mother* to be patient and compassionate, to trust and become empty, so that a path can be found. These humans are a young race, but their potential is vast. We will find a way, my sister. These humans together are the left brain of *Gaia*, and we are the right brain. The *Earth Mother* needs us both. Wounded and dangerous they may be, but they are still her children."

From the darkness of the earth, and from across the seven seas, their songs became louder, moving through the meridians of *Gaia*, renewing the strands that were broken, singing a song of hope and freedom. I felt an energetic transmission entering my body from behind the back of my head, and found myself expanding deeper and further out than I had ever experienced before.

I became the whales, I became the ocean, I became the earth. I was no longer a tiny human walking upon the face of the earth, but the living body of the earth herself. And then I found myself expanding out to become the size of an entire universe, experiencing the entire planet as a tiny wave inside the totality of a vast inter-connected presence. I could feel the *Mother* inside me stronger than I had ever felt before. The scales began to return to a point of balance, and then finally tipped over to become lighter than the feather.

"You have accomplished a great thing today, Elmira," I heard the song of a white whale speaking within me. "We would not have remained on this earth long if the humans had been destroyed," they said. "We are shepherds for the collective human soul, even if they do not know this or ask for this. What we are collectively experiencing today is the turning away from the density of *Kali Yuga*, and a slow ascent into an *Age of Light*." I felt her then entering my multi-dimensional field, allowing me access to the heart of the universe.

Sekhmet came then to embrace me. "You cannot imagine how I felt after accomplishing my task that day after Anubis showed me the future of the earth. I wanted to die a thousand deaths. As a mother I know how to protect my own cubs, but instead I condemned so many to their deaths. I went berserk that day, only to become like those who go mad with their own acts of plundering." A white lion came towards me, and entered my vision center. "You have shown me a different way, Elmira. Know I will always walk by your side."

Anubis came to me then, head bowed before me. "You have vanquished me, my daughter. My task through all these years has been to provide stern justice for souls who had lost their way. But you have created within the underworld a path to light, born of mercy, and your loyalty to the *Great Mother*." A white wolf came to stand by me then, and entered my belly, "Congratulations, my child," continued Anubis, "You have learned to follow your truth no matter what, and have helped me find a deeper truth as well."

He took his great pair of scales and broke them in front of my eyes. "These are not needed anymore," he announced. "From this day forward, the light of the *Mother* will be available for all those who have died. I still fear that humans will one day destroy the body of this Earth, but that responsibility is no longer mine." Tenderly, he took the white feather of justice and placed it into my hands. "The fate of the earth belongs to you now, and others like you. Keep this in your heart, Child of the Stars. Guard it well."

And then I heard the granite lid above the sarcophagus being removed, and hands slowly lifted me out from the enclosed space. Three days had passed since I had entered. Aisha massaged my stiff body, and took me into her arms, tears streaming down her face. "I thought I had lost you, my beautiful daughter. I tried to follow you there at the end, but was not allowed to. The *Earth Mother* said you needed to do that last part on your own."

"And then the whales came, and they helped you with their soothing songs, and created with you a path of return. I am so proud of you, my child. You stayed in the purity of your heart, and held strong your truth through the darkness of endless ages. You have accomplished what none of us have been able to. You have shattered the realms of the underworld, which has trapped the souls of humanity within this dark matrix of duality for so many long eons!"

And then my mother Mirjan was standing by my side, holding me tight, along with Issa and Chetan Nath, and Thoth and Aranyani, and all the guardians within the sacred temple of Shambala. They looked exhausted, for each of them too had been tested to their limits. But there was tenderness and joy reflected in each pair of eyes as we joined hands together in one big circle, and sang a song of celebration and freedom for *Mother Gaia*.

Chapter 49

Mirra Alfassa

Sometimes a great wandering thought moves across the vast ocean of time, and finds fulfilment in ages yet to come. It finds an echo in times of darkness when extinction seems the only possible choice. It creates a wormhole between dimensions where the breath of the dragons opens a door to timelines that existed not before.

And so it was with that promise I made to Anubis, when I swore to move earth and heaven itself so that humanity might fulfil the task they had been given.

An avatar is one who pierces through dimensions and seeds new waves of possibility from beyond the causal flow of history. It is the descent of pure consciousness across the veils of space and time to birth itself within the field of matter. And so it was that in response to that call, and in response to a great longing at the heart of humanity, Shiva chose a human embodiment to bring into fulfilment what was already destined to be.

In a city known in India as Kolkata, a young boy took birth in 1872. Yes, I am jumping around in time once again, and we are now in a period very close to what you will be experiencing as the *shift of the ages*. He was named Aravinda, which means *lotus*. True to his name, his task was to create the conditions for a new race of humanity to emerge from the muddy depths of the unconscious, a race that could embody the power of the ancient gods.

His early life was spent in England, which had become a colonial empire by then. It was an England that had lost its magic, and thought to gain it back through conquest and enslavement. Aravinda's role at that time was to fan the flames of independence and freedom for the land of his birth, which had lost its sovereignty to England, but still somehow managed to retain its spiritual integrity.

It wasn't long before his vision expanded beyond national independence to something vaster and far more inclusive. It was not just a revolt against the British empire, but a revolt against the fallen nature of humanity, that his soul naturally gravitated towards. Inspired by luminaries who had been practicing the path of yogic union, he soon managed to pierce the veils of existence, realizing himself as infinite consciousness, and recognizing that the path to humanity's freedom was now at hand.

It was about this time that I came into embodiment as well. I have explained earlier that from the perspective of soul there is neither time nor separation. So it is not a contradiction that I could retain an immortal body as *manu* for the sixth root race, while still incarnating as the power of *shakti* to serve this incarnation of *Shiva*.

The year was 1878. A child was born in Paris, France, to a Turkish father and Egyptian mother, whom I successfully joined consciousness with. I was named Mirra Alfassa. Since I continued to maintain my connection as Elmira, this child was able to incarnate without the customary veils. I understood from the time I was very young that my task was to serve as a bridge between the worlds, and to support Aravinda in the task of human liberation.

A child does not immediately remember the totality of its being. As with all humans, there is a slow process of physical and intellectual development, until the moment when he or she is ready to become initiated into a deeper memory of self. And so it was that just as Aravinda was triggered into his awakening by a visiting yogi, I too became apprenticed to an occultist in order to gradually reactivate my inner knowing.

I grew into a vibrant young woman with a passion for sports, art and nature, and with the ability to enter the consciousness of flowers as a mirror for emerging gifts within humanity. I married, travelled, even gave birth to a son when I was twenty, all the while knowing that in the fulness of time I would be meeting my Krishna, this purest of souls, so that together we could fulfil the path of my destiny.

Chapter 50

The Meeting

The year was 1914. The first great war of the 20th century had just begun. I was with my second husband then. The world was on the precipice of change. Anubis had shown up unbidden with a vision of the horrors and turmoil that lay ahead for the world, reminding me of the feather I still carried in my heart, and the promise I had made to the *Earth Mother*.

Meanwhile, I had been seeing in my dreams the man I was destined to meet, showing up on top of a spiraling staircase in an old colonial home, overlooking a spacious courtyard somewhere on the eastern coast of India. Was I ready to go seek him out?

It was my husband who made the decision for me. I was in my mid-thirties at the time, and he decided to move to Pondicherry, India, which was a French colony at the time, in order to pursue his political ambitions. Although he did not accomplish his goals, it was here that I met the Krishna of my dreams. Radiating an extraordinary combination of serenity and passion, I recognized in Sri Aurobindo, as he was then being called, the north star of my inner landscape.

Everything stopped for me at that point. We both recognized in each other the one we had come to fulfil a destiny with. No, it is not like some of you may be imagining. It was not a sexual or romantic attraction, but something far deeper, and much more powerful. It was the primal attraction of *shiva* and *shakti,* an awakening of memory from beyond the subtlest realms of creation. It was a recognition that the time had come to bring heaven down to earth, awakening the divinity dormant in each cell of physical consciousness.

I must say a little more about the magnetic attraction that brings two beings together. When two people are each only partially awake, they look for their awakening within the other. It is an attraction of opposites, usually accompanied with great intensity, instability, drama, and emotion. People refer to this as *falling in love,* and they can just as quickly fall out of love when this projection is removed.

But when each person has evolved to the point where they experience a balance between the inner masculine and inner feminine, there is no more projection. There is only the mirroring of souls. A quality of magnetic resonance is created which empties out the last shreds of personal self, and pierces the doors of infinity with the power of soul resonance. They begin to transcend the illusions of the personal ego, the dualities of human experience, and the conditioning of the human mind.

I call this *rising in love,* and it has nothing to do with physical attraction. It happens after you have become familiar with the dark nights of the soul, when you no longer need to escape or hide from the depths of your own being, and when you are ready to fulfil the soul purpose for which you have come to this earth. And so it was that my meeting with Sri Aurobindo initiated ancient soul memories from beyond the veils of creation, sparking within both of us an evolutionary impulse that would eventually lead to the advent of a new humanity.

You will remember, in *Daughter of the Moon,* that Mirjan refers to levels of the mind beyond rational thought, and how Aisha's ability to travel through these *tattwas* was the necessary bridge to emerge safely from her journey to the underworld, and subsequently build her body of light.

Likewise, in the journey of collective embodiment, Sri Aurobindo had mapped out this same inner landscape, creating a ladder from the rational mind up towards primordial consciousness through various levels of mental consciousness which he identified as the *higher mind*, the *illumined mind*, the *intuitive mind*, the *overmind*, and finally the *supermind*.

Our task was to climb this ladder, touch the oceans of infinity existing beyond the five veils of *maya*, and bring this down through all the intervening *tattwas* and dimensions into the deepest heart of matter. It would mean ascending into the realm of primordial consciousness, and then descending into the underworld of matter, transforming this cellular matrix into a womb for new creation.

The yoga that Sri Aurobindo had developed, much like what I had been taught by my own teachers, was not about transcendence but rather embodiment. Soon, a circle of disciples began to grow around us. The yoga we taught became known as Integral Yoga, an approach to spiritual evolution that aimed to integrate all aspects of human existence, physical, mental, emotional and spiritual, into a harmonious whole.

It was not about withdrawal from the activities of life, but the transformation of every aspect of human existence. The goal was to become empty enough so that the *supramental force* could take hold of the five koshas and use them for its own evolutionary purpose.

Chapter 51

Supramental Descent

What are the levels of mind that Sri Aurobindo had so carefully mapped? The *higher mind* learns to develop a bird's eye view, see the big picture, and move out from a causal perspective of reality into a synchronistic experience of life. You have learned to become empty of emotional bias, and developed a quality of discernment. Decisions made from this level of the mind transcend linear thinking, and touch a level of intuitive truth beyond the confines of rational thought.

Once you learn to touch this intuitive truth, the power of soul begins to move through your senses. You have emptied out your third-dimensional perceptions of reality, and you begin to open to other dimensions, including what you might call the clairvoyant, clairaudient and clairsentient realms. Your spiritual eye has become integrated with the physical eyes, you are listening to the sounds of creation, you are feeling the pulse of a universal force. This is the realm of the *illumined mind.*

Once you learn to expand your sensory range, you can now begin to move past the illusion of separation. You have emptied yourself from ideas of a personal self. You look at a person, and you become that person, you look at a flower and you become that flower. You are seeing them as if you are inside them, and they are inside you. This level of mind has been termed the *intuitive mind*. Do not confuse this with ordinary intuition. It is rather a level of perception where you have learned to see past the outer form into the primal essence.

Beyond this is an archetypal realm where you have become empty of any definitions of human identity. You are no longer subject to the *saturnian matrix* that we spoke about earlier, no longer attached to a single dimension of reality. Like the whales, you find yourself shifting through dimensions, able to access information from anywhere within the akashic worlds. This is the realm of the gods and goddesses, the realm of the *overmind*.

It is a level of mind that very few people have learned to access. But there is a level of mind that goes even further, which Sri Aurobindo termed the *supermind*. Here you have become empty of the *kanchukas*, and experience yourself as creator within the dance of creation. You have become the mind of the universe, pouring in through your multi-dimensional experience of Self to fluidly shape and influence all levels of reality, including the worlds of physical matter.

The intention that I had voiced in the underworld of Anubis, the promise I had made to bring an errant human race into maturity, had come not from the personal self but from the heart of creation itself. This intention has always remained dormant within the depths of matter, which is also the heart of the *Universal Mother*.

This is the potential that *Gaia* seeks to fulfil, which is why she has chosen to evolve such an incredible diversity of life, including human. The human species has gradually evolved past the *animal human*, where the urge to growth came from an instinctive urge for self-preservation, to the *human human*, where we learned to experience and shape reality through the mind.

We are now moving towards the *divine human*, where the soul begins to harmonize with the mind. This is the foundation of the sixth root race, or *homo luminous*. This will be followed by a seventh root race, *homo universalis*, where the knowledge of Self permeates all aspects of being, including matter itself.

This is the work I had come to fulfil, along with Sri Aurobindo. We referred to this as the *supramental descent*. It would happen in stages. The supramental force would first need to descend into the overmental consciousness of humanity, then into mental consciousness, and finally into biological consciousness.

The descent into the overmental planes has already taken place. It is something that Sri Aurobindo accomplished on behalf of humanity in 1926, after which he went into complete seclusion, leaving me in charge of the ashram. I became known as *the Mother* from this time onwards, an earthly embodiment of the *Divine Mother*, and continued the work of anchoring this force into the mental consciousness of humanity.

Whenever there is a level of supramental descent, however, there is resistance from the darkness of a collective underworld. Another Great War broke out in 1939 as collective shadows broke towards the surface, threatening to almost engulf the work we had begun. With the support of all those who had joined us in this work, and with the collective heart of a humanity learning to embrace and heal these shadows, the work continued. The horrors of war and human degradation could no longer be tolerated, and humanity began to wake up.

The next phase was the descent of supramental force into the physical planes. We realized that we were not strong enough to accomplish this as long as we both remained in the physical planes, that one of us would need to create a polarity from a higher dimension of consciousness.

Since I had access to my immortal body, and had already experienced the human underworld, it was decided that Sri Aurobindo would be the one to depart the physical body, which he did in 1950, to continue the work from higher realms. I took on his etheric mantle, just as my mother had received the etheric mantle of Aisha, to continue the work more effectively.

Chapter 52

Supramental Catastrophe

The work continued. The descent of supramental force into the physical planes was finally accomplished on February 29, 1956. I wrote in my journal that day:

"This evening the Divine Presence, concrete and material, was there present amongst you. I had a form of living gold, bigger than the universe, and I was facing a huge and massive golden door which separated the world from the Divine. As I looked at the door, I knew and willed, in a single movement of consciousness, that 'the time has come', and lifting with both hand a mighty golden hammer I struck one blow, one single blow on the door, and the door was shattered to pieces. Then the supramental Light and Force and Consciousness rushed down upon earth in an uninterrupted flow."

For the first time on that day, the supramental Light and Force entered the physical world. It initiated a new phase of human and planetary evolution, the first step to fulfilling my promise to Anubis. It will take some time for this new earth consciousness to infiltrate into all the structures and systems governing your planet, but this descent of the supramental was a decisive step, perhaps one of the most important events in many cycles of history.

There is a downside to this work, however. As supramental light enters ever more deeply into the shadows of the human underworld, it forces everything that is buried and unacknowledged up to the surface. Sri Aurobindo recognized this would happen, and referred to this process as the *supramental catastrophe*. What this means is that before the final moment of awakening, there would be a period of time when things would feel increasingly desperate and chaotic.

During this stage, it might look like there is an immense battle between forces of good and evil playing itself out on all levels. From the perspective of duality, this may be true. But from a higher perspective, it is merely a process of increasingly powerful light unveiling the last traces of hidden darkness. Sri Aurobindo made it very clear that the *supramental catastrophe* does not refer to destruction or extinction. There is a unifying force even in the darkest moments capable of holding things together as illusions fall apart.

There is much written about the work of *supramental descent*, which you can discover for yourself if you search for it. There have also been many study circles and communities which have emerged around this vision, including Auroville, a city for human unity which I founded in 1968, shortly before leaving that incarnation in 1973.

This work of supramental descent did not end with my departure however, and continues with each of you drawn to this work. You will know you are part of this mission by the resonance you feel in your heart and within your soul, and by the vibrancy you experience within your physical body. Each of you has a role to play, and will discover this as you continue to follow the path of your heart.

The full manifestation of this supramental descent will be completed soon, and will be synchronized with events such as the galactic superwave and magnetic reversal which I have spoken about earlier. It has already begun on levels of the overmind, and within the mental consciousness of humanity, although it has yet to play out fully within physical density.

A supramental world already exists in a timeline close to your own. A bridge connecting to this world also has been built. It is up to each of you now to walk across this bridge and experience this world within you.

The shift I am talking about will be extremely dramatic. As you enter a new timeline, there will be no room to wonder whether or not this has happened. As you walk across the bridge, many of you will yourselves in bodies that look different, and not as susceptible to ageing, disease or death. The need for external technologies will drop away as you discover a range of abilities never imagined before. As humanity goes through a collective shift, this will ripple out across all species of life, lifting the vibrational frequency of the entire planet into fourth density.

Some of you will even find yourself going past fourth density into fifth density, which is the equivalent of the seventh root race. This is the *gnostic* species that Sri Aurobindo spoke about, the birth of the superhuman.

I am aware that there is much talk in your times about a superhuman race emerging through advances in artificial intelligence. This has nothing to do with *gnosis*. What you call artificial intelligence is still essentially a product of the rational mind. It is only when you become aligned with higher levels of mind, an organic evolutionary process which is inevitable at this time, that you will understand the true potential of divinity expressed through a mature species of humanity.

Chapter 53

The Journey Ahead

All right, so this is Elmira again, or Mira as I prefer to be called. And yes, sometimes the presence of Mirra Alfassa comes through more actively, as when I was telling you about her story, and how she was able to set the stage, along with Sri Aurobindo, for root races still to come.

I want to give you a perspective now of how close this time actually is for those of you incarnated in the early 21st century, and the sequence of events leading up to this. Perhaps this will help you prepare for this Shift, and also help you see through some of the illusions of your times. It may seem like a paradox, but because of the nature of the supramental catastrophe, it may even seem for a while that you are going further into darkness rather than light.

Do not be surprised when you see an increase in wars, invasions, oppression, genocide, terror, deception, depravity and greed. These waves of darkness emerging from your collective underworld are a natural response to the supramental descent, and provide you with an opportunity to release your own dragons, choosing a way of truth, power and compassion.

You have inherited an upside-down world, where war is peace, slavery is freedom, and ignorance is strength. You are taught that the end always justifies the means, or rather, secret agendas always justify the lies. Truth became collateral damage in the great task of empire building. So what if it takes a few acts of genocide to found a great nation? So what if trusted patriarchs engage in deception to create a dominant religion? So what if a few more forest species go extinct in order to build a profitable economy?

As you move closer to the Shift you might find that on a collective level, mainstream lies become ever more blatant, discernment becomes increasingly difficult, and you are taught to unquestioningly swallow lies in allegiance to slavery of mind, body and soul. You would rather plunge into extinction than face your own truth. You would rather die in arrogance and illusion than take down the mask of your own collective dissonance.

On a personal level, however, many of you are waking up. Most people in the world today are not heartless tyrants and mindless consumers. You have learned to perceive yourselves as isolated and weak, but you are not soulless. You may be ignorant and misinformed, but you are not evil. Many of you are increasingly looking to give back to the earth, to make amends for past wrongs, and build a new world based on respect, sovereignty, justice and peace. You are looking to seek your truth, find your power, claim your freedom. These are all signs that the time of Shift is close at hand.

When I speak about the Shift, it is not a single event, but a sequence of events closely following each other, some of which have already begun. I will summarize this for you, and then describe each of these events more fully. Once you understand this, you will be able to walk through these times with joy and excitement, and to let go some of your fears when the roller coaster becomes more intense.

All right now, I will put on my teacher hat now, and share with you a general sequence of events relating to the Shift, although it may not be necessarily as linear as I am describing:

1. Cycle of the yugas

2. Galactic superwave

3. Heliopause breakthrough

4. Cosmic ray bombardment

5. Solar event

6. Magnetic Reversal

7. DMT Release

8. Crustal Plate Displacement

9. Dimensional Shift

10. Second Sun

11. Supramental Transformation

12. The Inconscient

13. Seventh universe

I have touched upon the mechanics of the magnetic reversal and related themes a few times earlier in this manuscript. Now it is time to go into these events a little bit deeper. This Shift we are referring to is not a single event but many. Scientists, mystics, and prophets have caught glimpses of this but never the full picture. I will do my best to describe this now as fully as I can.

Cycle of the Yugas

I have spoken often of the cycle of *Yugas* moving through a descending phase of light to darkness, and then an ascending phase from darkness to light. Is there a relationship between these Four Yugas, the Four Ages of the Greeks, and the Twelve Astrological Ages of the Chaldeans and Sumerians? What do they reveal not only about your ancient past but also events you might expect in the future, even within your own lifetime?

Each of these cycles span a period of 24,000 years, a wheel of life representing a journey of darkness and light, death and renewal. The transition between Ages is not always smooth. The crossing points between the Ages of Virgo and Leo, and also between the Ages of Pisces and Aquarius, are especially important, for sudden and dramatic shifts typically take place during this time, often accompanied by catastrophes involving flooding, tsunamis, earthquakes, volcanoes, and even *crustal plate displacements.*

You are in transition between the Age of Pisces and the Age of Aquarius right now. This corresponds to a point where you are moving out from the *Kali Yuga,* which is the phase of deepest inertia and density, into *Dwapara Yuga,* characterized by the first stage of the return journey, and the infusion of new energies into the planetary body. In the long history of your planet, you have experienced cycles of catastrophes every 12,000 years, sometimes also during a 6,000 year halfway point, often ending in an extinction event for much of planetary life.

What many people may not be aware of is that the *yugas* are directly related to your Sun's astronomical movement around its twin star, Sirius, as together they orbit around the center of your galaxy. The center of your galaxy represents a realm of higher dimensional light, which dissipates as you move away from the center. Thus, as these twin stars orbit around the center of the galaxy, whenever your own sun moves closer to the galactic center you move into an age of light, while every time you move further away you pass through an age of darkness.

Does it surprise you then that Ages of Light were associated with wisdom, knowledge, self-awareness, longevity, culture, and marvels of technology? As your Sun moved away from the galactic center, the path of self-knowledge became a dim memory, culture degraded, knowledge dissolved into dogma, and the technological and archaeological wonders of an ancient past were lost and forgotten. Gods became demi-gods who became mortals.

How many of you worry that the cycle of wars will never end, that a small group of psychopaths will end up ruling the world? How many of you have wondered what you are doing on this planet, despairing of your ability to make a difference? How many of you have carried the weight of the world on your shoulders, burdened under the anguish of human suffering?

The cycle of suffering has become deeply ingrained during the past 6000 years of *kali yuga*. But it is time to remember a time before this, when you could feel the power of creation moving through you, when architectural feats were commonplace, when your human lifetime extended to more than a thousand years, when you could access all knowledge directly from the akashic records, when inner technologies had more value than external technologies, when love was the only currency of exchange that was needed.

Nothing is lost forever, however, for everything is preserved in akashic memory. These are the memories you are beginning to recover now, as you pass through the doorway of awakening. Ultimately you will find yourself moving back out through the veils of *maya*, releasing the illusions of limitation that keeps you trapped in third density, and back into an Age of Light.

The passage across the Ages is not linear. It may seem that you get stuck in a *kali yuga* for an interminable age, because it is a density where time is experienced as linear. As you move towards the *satya yuga*, however, you begin to enter into fourth and fifth densities where time moves differently, just like Hiranya experienced among the Tuatha de Danann, and various timelines or time bubbles begin to operate. Thus, each time you move into an Age of Light you are experiencing not just the ending of a cycle but a spiral of ever new possibilities.

Thus, it is possible that you may not need to experience the scale of catastrophe that you have experienced in past transitions. Although you have already made this choice on a collective level, supported by the supramental energies that are now beginning to move through your planetary experience, many of you are still sitting on the fence regarding personal choices you will be making. Which timeline will you choose for yourself?

There is one more thing about the *yugas* that is important to understand. There is an additional cycle of *yugas* that covers the orbit of your solar system around the galactic center. This is a much larger orbit, taking approximately 230 million years to complete, crossing through many different densities along the way, and is referred to as a Galactic Year.

Your own galaxy meanwhile is also in orbit around a Super-Galactic Center, which in turn is being pulled towards a region in space known as the Great Attractor. With all these factors in play, it must become obvious to you now that no two cycles are ever the same. With the descent of supramental light into the density of matter, an entirely new realm of possibilities is becoming available now, which I will share more about later.

Chapter 55

Galactic Superwave

All right then, we've talked about the *yugas*, and that this includes a descending cycle of 12,000 years followed by an ascending cycle of 12,000 years, for a total of 24,000 years. This has to do with the orbit of your sun around its twin star.

So, starting with these two suns orbiting around each other, let's move out to the very center of your galaxy, which has a gravitational energy millions of times larger than your own sun. Your astronomers sometimes refer to this as a *black hole*, but this is not true. In the center of your galaxy, as with all spiral galaxies, is a pulsating *mother star*, which you could call a *white hole* if you wish, and which sends out periodic bursts of ionized particles across the entire Milky Way galaxy.

There has never been a single 'big bang' as some of your scientists claim. The universe is in a state of continuous creation. This creative force emanates out from the center of galaxies in the form of *galactic superwaves*, composed of cosmic and gamma rays vibrating at extremely high frequencies.

These cosmic rays are carrier waves for evolutionary information. When these superwaves interact with solar systems and planets, the magnetic fields associated with matter absorb this information, and new potentials are made available for genetic repatterning and the creation of new species.

It is like dropping a pebble into the center of a still pond and watching the waves move out in a circular pattern. In this case, galactic waves, spaced 12,000 years apart, move out across the galactic equator, passing through all matter encountered along the way, carrying galactic information for seeding and supporting a next evolutionary cycle.

Like the periodicity of an ascending or descending yuga cycle, a galactic superwave thus passes through your solar system every 12,000 years, carrying with it information that can radically alter life on your planet. Note that it is the same periodicity of 12,000 years.

Galactic superwaves are synchronized with all major cycles within the Milky Way, including solar cycles, the timing of magnetic reversals on earth, and even cycles of catastrophe. Each galaxy is entrained to the steady rhythm of a galactic heartbeat, linked with other galaxies across the universe through a plasma network known esoterically as Indra's Net.

So, I have a question for you. If there are packets of galactic information riding in on cosmic rays pouring in through your weakening magnetic fields, what does it mean for humans, and other life on this planet? What does it mean in terms of *Gaia's* evolutionary journey? Could it be that incoming cosmic rays, besides having physical effects on atmospheric and seismic patterns, could also have a biological effect on planetary ecosystems? How do you think this might be related to the supramental descent we spoke about earlier?

The extinction of species, and the creation of new species, seem to go together in times of geomagnetic collapse and reversal. Could this be related to the advent of a galactic superwave? What are the mechanisms for this? Could this be linked to cycles of catastrophe where much of life is periodically destroyed, followed by the activation of new genetic pathways, as new potentials are activated through incoming packets of information?

Your scientists are able to track the passage of this superwave as it approaches your solar system by measuring its effects on stars along the way. You are on the verge of receiving the next superwave pulse. So I have another question for you. What does it mean that this galactic superwave is approaching your solar system at this transition between the Kali Yuga and Dwapara Yuga?

If each *yuga* lasts 3000 years in your ascending journey of light, this entry into *dwapara yuga* signifies a birthing process. It will be another 6000 years until you emerge into the *satya yuga,* but this transition is very significant. Some astrologers calculate that you will be entering the Aquarian Age beginning March 21, 2025.

If the Kali Yuga is about density and inertia, the Dwapara Yuga is about movement and energy. You have been going through a time when alternate forms of energy are being made available to you, not only through harnessing the power of the sun, wind and waves, but also through a new understanding of cosmic energy.

The power of atomic energy you have learned to release, immense though it may be, is still insignificant when compared to the power inherent within these cosmic waves. Are you evolved enough to safely handle these energies? An entire root race of humanity was destroyed 12,000 years ago because they had learned to develop the power of atomic and cosmic energy, but not the ability to use this wisely.

Chapter 56

Heliopause Breakthrough

And so, like a stern schoolmaster, I will ask this question once more. *Are you ready to open Pandora's Box again?* Two timelines stretch out before you, and the choice is yours.

What are these two timelines? If you have allowed yourself time to ponder over my question, you will understand that I am referring to both personal and collective choices. Up until recently, you had made your bed in a pile of muck, choosing to lie in it, suffocating in your own wastes, as great waves gathered to take you down again.

With the descent of supramental force, another timeline has now opened up before you. This does not mean that all of you will choose this, nor that the path ahead will be easy. But it does mean that massive earth changes and catastrophic extinction is not the only choice available to you anymore.

These two timelines are linked with different vibrational densities, and can be described simply as third density and fourth density realities. As primordial light continues to anchor into the physical and mental planes of your planet, the meridians and leylines use this supramental force to strengthen the Earth's grids and eventually shift from one density to another.

Are you familiar with what a quantum shift looks like? On the microcosmic level, electrons orbit around the nucleus of every atom in distinct orbits. As you add energy, either in the form of heat or in the form of light, there comes a point when electrons from a lower orbit suddenly jump to the next orbit above. The same thing happens on your journey from third density to fourth density.

All right, we will come back to all this, but let's first talk about what will happen when the galactic superwave initially touches the boundary of your solar system.

There is a skin around your solar system, just like the protective magnetic shield around the earth, which is able to shrink and expand according to solar or galactic influences. This skin, known to your scientists as the *heliopause*, is composed of highly charged ionized particles, or plasma, creating a shield of protection against an unruly swarm of cosmic dust, comets and asteroids floating about in your journey through galactic space.

Like a lagoon of still water protected by reefs while great waves surge in a vast ocean beyond, this heliopause also protects your solar system from the intensity of the galactic superwave as it moves your way. But there comes a time when the impact is too strong and too sustained, and the shield breaks down.

At this point, huge quantities of cosmic and gamma rays enter your solar system, along with millions of tons of dust and debris normally held outside this protective shield. Most of the debris is gravitationally attracted by the Sun and by larger planets such as Jupiter and Saturn. Some of it moves into the inner solar system, creating havoc with magnetic fields and tides. Sometimes comets slam into the surface of a planet, such as the one that contributed to a great catastrophe on Earth 12,000 years ago.

You must understand that your Sun is not an isolated body in the fabric of space. It is energetically linked to other stars across the galaxy through invisible fields of plasma. What happens when plasma from the galactic center as well as dust and debris from outer space bombard the surface of the Sun?

Your Sun has its own cycles, just like the Earth and other planets, each of them entrained to the galactic pulse. Sometimes it is a red giant, other times a mellow yellow, other times a white dwarf. While this is easily seen in the bigger scale of time, it is also seen on a smaller scale within the 12,000-year cycle of galactic pulsing.

The galactic pulse contributes to cycles of warming and cooling on earth and other planets, along with atmospheric changes, pole shifts, and magnetic reversals. The outer planets in your solar system have already gone through many of these shifts. Similar phenomena will soon be experienced upon the Earth, the timing of which will depend on when exactly you make the shift between the *kali yuga* and *dwapara yuga*.

I have spoken about the impact of cosmic dust and cometary debris upon your solar system as the plasma shield around your solar system breaks down. The incoming cosmic rays and gamma rays will also directly impact all aspects of consciousness upon the Earth.

Chapter 57

Cosmic Ray Bombardment

Many of you are beginning to experience the impact of ionized plasma from the galactic center, which is also the carrier for supramental light entering from a supra-galactic source, as a sort of *cosmic electricity,* or *divine fire.* Your life force energies, or *kundalini shakti* is being stimulated as never before.

It is a two-edged sword. When you are in a state of balance, this fire helps burn away the subconscious veils of *maya,* your senses awaken, and your access to multi-dimensional consciousness becomes effortless. When you are not in balance, this same fire triggers deeply held patterns of resistance, which rise to the surface seeking release.

This is why some of among you are waking up so quickly now, while others are moving into a time of increasing fear, aggression, confusion and anguish. There are prophecies in all your religions about waves of *purification.* The Inkas spoke of *pachakuti,* the Norse spoke about the *ragnarok,* the early Christians spoke about an *apocalypse,* the Muslims spoke about *qiyamat,* and our rishis spoke about the *pralaya.*

They all point to an immense wave of cosmic electricity entering from cosmic space and engulfing the earth. They are referring to a time of purification when everything gets turned upside down, both figuratively and literally. Do not forget what happened with Atlantis 12,000 years ago, when a combination of tectonic activity, volcanoes, giant tsunamis and crustal plate displacement destroyed an entire civilization. Earthquakes and volcanoes are directly related to an increase in cosmic ray activity.

The choice before you has to do with the two timelines you currently face. Either everything around you will collapse and disappear, nothing being left of this civilization with its perversity and willful ignorance, or you will allow this fire to rejuvenate, purify, and reconstruct everything. Matter will be refined, and your hearts liberated from ignorance and anguish. This is the other side of the *supramental catastrophe.*

I have shared with you my journey into the underworld, and the challenge I faced with Anubis. Subsequently, in my incarnation as Mirra Alfassa I managed to open a path of return, where the descent of supramental light was able to create a new timeline for humanity and the Earth.

But just because a path exists does not mean that you have to take it. The choice still exists for each of you. Do you wish to remain in the prison of your own mind, walking on a treadmill of existential suffering, as in the dream I had shared earlier? Your ability to survive and thrive depends on how willing you are to receive the intensity of this light, and to be transformed by it.

How will these cosmic rays affect your physical bodies, your nervous systems, your alignment between heart, mind, soul and spirit? How will they affect your collective journey of awakening? How will they affect the physical body of the Earth, particularly in reference to spikes in tectonic and volcanic activity, jet streams, cloud formation, warming and cooling cycles? How will this *divine fire* support your ascent towards the sixth root race?

For most of you reading this, you have already been doing the inner work necessary to integrate this divine fire. However, on the collective level, you must know that there has been a deliberate agenda for global enslavement and control active within your political, banking, medical, military, agricultural and industrial systems for the past many decades. Most wars being fought in your world today are simply about maintaining this agenda.

I need not go into the details of this right now, except to affirm that none of these devious agendas will be allowed to succeed. This cosmic electricity is sweeping across the world faster than any virus ever could, and people are waking up. The time of liberation ahead will be as lightning across a darkened sky. Only those who walk the ways of love, respect, honor and compassion will be invited to remain on this earth. Those who refuse to wake up will find themselves facing a disaster of their own making.

The entry of cosmic rays has only just begun. As the power of the incoming galactic superwave enters its totality, there will be much bigger waves of cosmic electricity to come, some of which will also trigger events of great intensity within the sun. The vibrational frequency you have managed to anchor by this time will determine how you experience these events.

Chapter 58

Solar Events

There are three cycles generated by the Sun which I want to elaborate on now. The first is the 11-year sunspot cycle, including a point of solar maximum and solar minimum at the halfway points of this period. There is also a grand solar maximum and grand solar minimum, comprised of a series of 36 sunspot cycles, repeating itself every 400 years, and causing what is known as a Little Ice Age during the low points of this cycle.

Finally, you have a 12,000-year cycle of coronal mass ejections, also known as a *solar micronova*. The penetration of the heliopause, and subsequent increase of electrical activity within the Sun, is followed shortly afterwards by the entire outer shell of the Sun being ejected out into space.

Micronovas are weaker than novas, which take place at the end of a star's life, but are still powerful enough to send out highly ionized solar winds across the solar system. These winds are capable of penetrating the magnetic shields protecting each planet, creating the magnetic reversals I have referred to earlier.

On the Sun, there are magnetic reversals taking place every 11 years, related to sunspot activity. As I have said before, your Sun is not a separate entity that sustains itself through radiant heat. It is linked through sheets of electromagnetic forces to an infinite tapestry of suns, planets and galaxies, all synchronized together through a universal heartbeat.

In response to the periodic entry of a *galactic superwave*, your Sun goes through an electromagnetic spike which allows it to synchronize more deeply with this universal heartbeat. The solar winds which move out following a solar micronova are thus linked with subtle informational fields that support the further evolution of each planet.

Solar micronovas are capable of generating the *cosmic electricity* which I referred to earlier, accompanied by consciousness changes and earth changes. So, there are waves of cosmic electricity linked with cosmic and gamma ray bursts emanating from the galactic center, and also waves of cosmic electricity linked with solar winds emanating from your Sun. They may follow each other, or they could be simultaneous, but at a certain point will cause a sudden reversal of your planetary magnetic field.

I will give you a hint. The exact timing for the breakdown of the heliopause, and thus also for the solar micronova, could well be related to the next *grand solar minimum*, which you will be experiencing soon. Prepare for some extreme cold weather during this time. Meanwhile, as your Sun goes into a grand solar minimum, the solar wind decreases, which in turn weakens the electromagnetic shield surrounding your solar system, allowing radiation from the galactic superwave to break through, initiating a solar micronova.

There is another type of solar event which is important to consider. Although not as strong as coronal mass ejections accompanying a solar micronova, your Sun periodically emits electrical flares which can project far out into inter-planetary space. Your scientists measure them according to their intensity as A, B, C, M and X, with A class flares being the weakest and X class flares being the strongest.

Because the protective magnetic field surrounding your Earth has been going through a weakening phase already, even an M class flare, if pointed directly towards you, can significantly impact the electrical power grids of your planet. Your current civilization has become heavily dependent on these power grids. What would happen if this went down completely, perhaps even permanently? What would happen to your systems of banking, food production, transportation and information exchange?

You have circuit breakers in your electrical power systems to protect you from destructive surges of power. Perhaps you can imagine this kind of solar flare to be a circuit breaker in your global systems of power if oppressive energies moving through the *saturnian matrix*, concentrated through the power of your *Deep State*, become too overwhelming.

This could be the first event in a series of dominoes leading up to the Shift. As you can imagine, a great deal of chaos would follow such an event, and you will need to prepare for this as best you can.

Chapter 59

Magnetic Reversal

All right then, so I have been sharing with you a sequence of events starting with the incoming *galactic superwave*. The collapse of the Earth's magnetic field is a key element within this sequence, and it is time to talk about this in more detail.

The Earth's magnetic field, synchronized with cycles within your Sun, is linked to the same universal heartbeat. Your magnetic poles weaken, collapse, and reverse every 12,000 years. Your geomagnetic field has been weakening significantly within the past 200 years, and also shifting position relative to the geographical poles. What will happen when the magnetic field collapses to zero, or when the magnetic polarity lines up in a new stable direction relative to its current position?

The collapse of the Earth's geomagnetic field is exponential, meaning that it starts slowly and then gets faster and faster. At the bottom of the reversal, synchronized with the *solar micronova*, there will be a brief moment of time that could last anywhere from a few hours to a few days, where the magnetic field of the Earth completely collapses and then realigns in the opposite direction. What happens during this time? And how far are you from experiencing this?

Is this the *three days of darkness* in Mayan prophecy?

Magnetic reversals have shaped planetary history for thousands of years. The *three days of darkness* spoken in various prophetic and mystical traditions offer humanity the choice of experiencing either an extinction or an evolutionary leap. I want to emphasize that it is a collective choice as well as a personal choice. If you resist the higher frequencies of soul, you may find ourselves leaving the physical body behind. But to the extent that you are willing to walk through this dark night, you will find yourself entering a multi-dimensional reality, followed by a new cycle of planetary evolution.

This is the New Earth consciousness that the Mayan, Inka and other indigenous prophecies have been pointing you towards, which saints and mystics around the world have consistently spoken about. The vibrational frequency of your planet is already shifting in response to the descent of supramental light, and in response to cosmic and galactic rays entering your solar system. These cosmic rays are already charging your cellular bodies in preparation for the magnetic reversal.

When does this magnetic reversal take place? Many of you are already preparing for this on a spiritual level. Many of you are going through kundalini activations, soul initiations, near death experiences, as well as encounters with galactic beings, elemental creatures, and *Gaia* herself.

All this is part of the preparation. You can also measure this event from a mathematical perspective, based on the changes being experienced in your geomagnetic fields, as well as incoming galactic superwaves and solar winds. I am not allowed to give you an exact date but I will say there is a 20 – or 22-year window between the advent of the Aquarian Age in 2025 and the completion of the birthing process. It will most likely happen during a solar minimum at the bottom of a grand solar minimum.

Since you are holographically connected with all dimensions of time and space within the universe, it is possible that an evolutionary leap on the scale that you are likely to experience on your planet will create a ripple effect across the entire fabric of time and space. Thus, for an advanced soul, these times of magnetic reversal are the most important times to incarnate in physical dimensions, which is why there are so many people here at this time. You have come here from across the vast universe, and what happens here affects the entire cosmos, perhaps because this planet is one of the densest as well as the most diverse of all planets.

During the three days of darkness, the magnetic field of the earth will collapse. Since it is this magnetic field that holds the five *koshas* together, this means that your physical, etheric, emotional, mental and soul bodies will temporarily disengage from each other, placing you in a state of suspended animation. You will be disconnected from the *saturnian matrix*, which is the repository for subconscious illusions of separation and fear.

Fear comes from the experience of existential separation, which is what this matrix is about. When the sense of separation dissolves, so does fear. This means that you will be able to go through a process of soul realignment without being influenced by the subconscious veils that normally govern your human experience.

You will go on your own journey through the underworld, just as many people experience during a *near death experience*. Afterwards, as the five sheaths reconstitute, you will find that the seat of consciousness is no longer centered around an illusory ego built from sub-conscious and mental conditioning, but around the expanded awareness of the soul.

Chapter 60

DMT Release

What happens during a near death experience?

There is a relationship between magnetic fields and a substance known as DMT, which is found within your pineal gland. Your human bio-systems are associated with magnetic fields which link your physical bodies to subtle and causal bodies beyond. This magnetic field, sometimes known as the *merkaba*, is centered around the heart. When the heart stops at the moment of physical death, this magnetic field breaks down. DMT is then released, which opens doorways to the upper worlds, so that the soul can exit its physical vehicle.

Let me emphasize this again. You are multi-dimensional beings trapped in the illusion of finiteness, limitation, and separateness. Your attention has become collectively fixated in an extremely restricted version of reality, where you imagine that who you are is a *personal self*, separate and distinct from everything else around you.

The truth, however, is that you are multi-dimensional beings inhabiting a multiple set of bodies, all of them linked together through the magnetic field of the Earth. So, what happens when the magnetic field of the Earth collapses? What happens to the relationship between these bodies?

Your five *koshas* are linked with corresponding levels of reality. Thus, your physical body is linked with physical dimensions of matter, your etheric body is linked with vital forces of nature, your mental body is linked with various regions of mind, your emotional body is linked with states of feeling and emotion, and your causal body is linked with the realms of your immortal Self. All these bodies are held together within the magnetic fields of *Gaia*. What happens when these bodies start decoupling from each other during the *three days of darkness*?

In a *near death experience,* you disconnect from the lower bodies and move out into the higher astral planes, releasing your identity with the human body, and experiencing yourself directly as the soul. When you are brought back, you retain a memory of who you are as the soul, allowing this awareness of universal identity to heal the wound of separation, entering into a new relationship with life based on unity rather than separation.

The same thing happens during physical death, except that in this case the soul releases the physical and etheric bodies, but continues to experience itself through an astral body and senses. In each case, the *merkaba*, which is the human magnetic aura centered around the heart, becomes deactivated, allowing the soul to leave.

When the magnetic aura around the heart collapses, a substance known as DMT is stimulated within the pineal gland which opens the doors of perception, allowing you to lift out of your physical bodies into astral and causal dimensions. This is the same substance found in plant medicines such as *soma* or *ayahuasca,* used in shamanic traditions to open doors of perception.

Here's the interesting part now. When the physical heart stops at death, the magnetic field surrounding the heart collapses, and DMT is activated. But there is another way that DMT can be activated, and this has to do with the collapse of the Earth's geomagnetic field.

What happens during a magnetic reversal when the five *koshas* disengage from each other, breaking their connection with the planetary *merkaba*?

Imagine the magnetic field of an entire planet being temporarily erased, including the underworld realms of the *saturnian matrix*. Imagine the entire world on a collective ayahuasca journey, laying the foundations for a massive evolutionary leap. It would be a collective near-death experience!

It has been demonstrated that people who have had a near death experience usually come back with a greatly enhanced sense of joy and presence. You are preparing to go through this collectively now. It is an opportunity for remembering who you are as infinite consciousness, while remaining involved within dimensions of matter.

Inka shamans referred to *homo luminous*, a new species of humanity capable of experiencing their multi-dimensionality while celebrating the beauty and diversity of the physical worlds. This is equivalent to the sixth root race I have been asked to initiate, the *sun-eyed children of a new dawn.*

Chapter 61

Crustal Plate Displacement

To the extent that you are able to connect with the multi-dimensional soul, these times have become more joyful and ecstatic than ever before. But to the extent that you feel trapped in a single dimension of time and space, your lives have become increasingly fearful. You find yourself experiencing fears around survival, fears around death, fears concerning loved ones who may be suffering or dying, fears around planetary or environmental extinction.

But once you understand that your existence here on this Earth is part of a much greater cycle of existence, once you understand that you can safely trust something beyond your limited perceptions of the self, then that fear begins to uncreate itself. It takes time to break out of the conditioning of separateness, but you are being given the experiences that you need in order to step into your sovereignty as well as your totality.

How many of you have had dreams about being engulfed in a giant tsunami? Or seeing the world go up in flames? How many of you have seen continents shift or mountains being brought down in an instant of time? These are not necessarily visions of the future, but memories that belong to an earlier cycle of catastrophe, including the last time your planet went through a magnetic reversal.

Due to the descent of supramental light into the physical body of the Earth, the impact of this next galactic superwave, followed by the solar micronova and magnetic reversal, will not be nearly as catastrophic as what happened with Atlantis. This is because you will be able to enter a new timeline this time around, and experience these events from a subtler dimension of matter which will be more fluid.

Twelve thousand years ago, the magnetic reversal on Earth was followed by a *crustal plate displacement*. The earth is composed of an inner core, an outer core, a mantle, lower crust and upper crust. The upper crust, which you live upon, extends for several hundred miles beneath the surface of the earth before it reaches the mantle. Under normal circumstances, the lower crust is locked into the mantle below.

However, when the geomagnetic field collapses during a magnetic reversal, this lower crust becomes liquefied, allowing the upper crust to slide directly over the mantle over massive distances. The weight of polar ice causes the earth to turn, allowing continents to sink, rise and move into new positions.

The intensity of this movement has a lot to do with the vibrational density of the Earth in that moment. The last time around, the Earth was getting ready to descend into Kali Yuga, and therefore needed to experience this shift on a very physical level. This is when Atlantis went down and the third density experiment began. If the Earth is sufficiently prepared for the Shift, however, then rather than going through a crustal mass displacement, *Gaia* can use the massive input of cosmic and solar energy to transition back into fourth density, and even beyond.

This is where you are now, and this is what I see taking place. At this point, the vibrational frequency of your planet will become more subtle, and matter itself will become more fluid. This ascension to a higher density does not mean leaving matter behind. Rather, as the old matrix is shattered, and false illusions no longer have the power to dominate human consciousness, you will find yourself entering more deeply into matter, able to make creative choices that were impossible before.

As my alter ego, Mirra, said in one of her talks, "The secret lies in matter. The supreme height touches the most material matter. All the splendors one can experience by going up, by getting out, by leaving, are nothing. They're *nothing*, they don't have that concrete reality. They seem vague compared to *here*. This is truly why the world has been created. It's in terrestrial matter, on Earth, that the supreme becomes perfected."

Chapter 62

Dimensional Shift

The human drama you have been experiencing lately is a necessary play of divine forces to accelerate your journey and emerge through these times with a 'minimum' of damage.

The same galactic wave is coming as with Atlantis earlier, the same solar micronova is happening again, the same cosmic radiation is pouring in, the same magnetic reversal will take place, but this time you will receive these energies through the consciousness of the supramental force. Instead of sinking under the waves like you did in Atlantis, you are rising into the paradigm of the *seventh universe*.

The difference this time has to do with the activity of the supramental force, your entry into *dwapara yuga*, and the mass awakening that is gradually taking place. The combination of these factors is creating a split within your current timelines. You are being given a choice now that didn't exist before.

There is a passage in the Christian Bible, attributed to Issa, that says, "Two men shall be working in the field, one gets taken and the other left behind. Two women will be grinding at the mill, one gets taken and the other left behind."

There are many interpretations of this, as with the rest of the Bible, much of which has been heavily edited over the centuries to fit the requirements of various emperors and theologians. But since I have the unique privilege of being able to go right to the source, I asked my father about this one day.

"They would surely crucify me all over again if I ever went back there," he chuckled. "They have built a doctrine about me returning from the clouds at the End of Days to snatch up those who believe in me while leaving the rest behind to be destroyed."

"But there is a certain truth to this," he asserted, and went on to remind me of the paradox known today as Schrödinger's Cat. "Two realities can co-exist beneath the surface of consciousness. But there comes a time when choices need to be made from a higher level of consciousness. When two timelines begin to diverge from each other it can be confusing for those who are caught in the middle, until they are ready to make a choice. This is what that parable is about. It is about finally making a choice."

"You have been given a collective choice between extinction and transformation," he went on to say, "and have chosen transformation. The universe is conforming to this choice now. But this does not mean that everyone needs to make this same choice on a personal level. Some may be too attached to the drama, or created too much personal karma, to let it all go at once, and may choose to continue their journey on a lower density planet. Others may choose to leave for the moment, but will come back in new bodies when they feel ready. Cataclysmic destruction could still happen, but only if this is the timeline you choose."

I can confirm this from my own experience with the supramental force. As you make a transition into fourth density, matter will become increasingly plastic, which means it will become increasingly responsive to your personal choices. Consensus reality does not apply here. The experience of fourth density is that many dimensions can co-exist, and two people can have two very different experiences while experiencing the same outer circumstances.

The supramental force has been quietly slipping in, and will permeate the entire consciousness of *Gaia* as you pass through the magnetic reversal. The ground has been prepared, the seeds have been sown, and the power of truth-consciousness has been working in the deep *inconscient* for some time now. It has a power and a purpose beyond what you know, and can transmute your planetary condition faster than you can imagine.

Your time is just beginning now, a purpose long awaited is being fulfilled. You each have a part to play in this as you surrender to the call of the *Divine Mother*. As She awakens within you, *Shiva* and *Shakti,* human and divine, are being revealed as one. The magnetic reversal is the doorway through which the gathering supramental force will permeate your earthly consciousness on all levels.

Rather than being an extinction event as in previous cycles, you will be propelled into a density where fifth and sixth dimensional worlds will open up for you. Earth humans, freed from shackles of slavery and duality, will join with tribes from the Inner Earth and from extra-terrestrial worlds, to create a galactic tribe. Some of you might choose to go yet further, and begin your journey towards the seventh root race.

Chapter 63

Second Sun

There seems to be growing interest in your own times about the Inka and Mayan prophecies. As I examine the Mayan tradition, I find a curious prophecy about a second sun rising up from the ocean immediately after the three days of darkness have passed. What is this about? Prophecies are often based on akashic memories, which wisdom keepers consult in order to predict future events. So what is the meaning of this double prophecy of three days of darkness followed by the rising of a second Sun?

Although it is describing a literal event, this prophecy cannot be interpreted from a third-dimensional perspective of reality. In order to understand what this prediction means, I will take you on a journey into the deepest layers of your subconscious mind, into the veil of illusion. As I have emphasized before, these veils exist within your own consciousness. It is not the world out there, but your interpretation of this world, based on subconscious structures of programming, that keep you trapped in perceptions of separation and duality.

The prophecy of the second sun is about uprooting this veil of illusion from the matrix of your cellular DNA. The frequency of this programming keeps you trapped in a third-dimensional perception of reality, which you consider the one and only reality of existence. The belief that third-dimensional reality is the only reality is itself the illusion, and you cannot make it through the Shift as long as this programming remains within your cells.

In context of your current civilization, the veil of illusion refers to your perception of the universe through mechanistic assumptions. What if the deeper implications of *plasma cosmology* begin to sink into your collective awareness, to shape a new biological species, reprogram subconscious beliefs about who you are and what is possible, overhaul your socio-economic and political systems, and transform your sciences and technologies in accordance with the requirements of *dwapara yuga*?

The prophecy of the *Second Sun* is linked with the *three days of darkness*. Think about what this means. When the geomagnetic field of the Earth collapses, which is what the three days of darkness is about, the collective matrix of personal identity begins to disintegrate. Your emotional and mental bodies are no longer tightly bound to old patterns of subconscious conditioning. You begin to unravel the dense veils that keep you trapped in third-dimensional density.

New potentials of genetic information become activated, which raises the frequency of the energy matrix vibrating the cells of your body, in turn helping you perceive realities beyond the narrow limits of your known physical senses. Your consciousness begins to merge with worlds and dimensions beyond third-dimensional matter. You open to subtler levels of the mind. You begin to anchor the multi-dimensional frequencies of the soul.

All this change happens very quickly during this time, as your sensory perceptions go into hibernation. Creative evolution is a quantum process that utilizes the enormous wave of incoming cosmic energy to shape new creation. In the absence of the subconscious conditioning that has trapped you within the veils of illusion for eons, you make a quantum jump of evolution into a new state of biological consciousness capable of integrating the multi-dimensional frequencies of your soul.

You can also interpret this prophecy of the Second Sun in a slightly different way. Most Suns exist as part of a binary star system. Your experience in this Solar System is unique in that you only perceive a single Sun. But what if your twin Sun has always existed on a higher octave of creation and you simply have not been able to see it?

What if it is not a second Sun entering your Solar System during this time of the Great Shift but rather your twin Sun becoming visible to you in this dimension, as your senses expand beyond the narrow limits imposed by linear consciousness?

Or what if this binary twin is Sirius, and you just haven't wrapped your minds around this yet? What if the advent of a Second Sun in your skies is the first visible sign of your emergence into *Dwapara Yuga*, and ultimately back into *Satya Yuga*, the *Age of Light*?

This new Sun is already manifested in spirit, say the Mayas. As you open to this radiance you will begin receiving and assimilating its energy in a direct way. Your bodies will be nourished directly from the energy of the new Sun.

You will learn to use the energy of this Sun to build internal technologies that directly resonate with your higher selves. You will learn to heal your bodies, and create new worlds. You will travel freely through multiple dimensions of the universe. You will nourish your bodies directly from fields of *prana* all around you. Outdated social, political, economic, and religious systems will fall away because they will no longer be needed.

As the veil of illusion dissolves, so too, does the subconscious matrix of fear, separation, and duality. You will experience this planet as a single interconnected consciousness unifying all things within the web of life. You will discover what it means to experience Creator-Consciousness within infinite dimensions of Creation!

The Mayas provide a reminder that the new Sun manifesting on the outside is a reflection of a new Sun being birthed within. This is the soul consciousness being birthed as you pass into the doorway of the new Earth!

It is the birth of a divine human, serving as a steward on this beautiful blue and green planet, inspired by a constantly flowing well of creative impulse. Rather than reacting instinctively in predetermined subconscious patterns, you will respond in each moment with the full intensity of your multi-dimensional presence, nurturing and honoring each strand in the web of planetary life.

Whatever is real from the old Earth will remain. Experiences that feed and enrich your souls, memories of beauty and love, all of these will remain. Nothing is ever lost in evolution. Old structures will be assimilated into higher octaves of reality. You will still experience the density of matter, simply vibrating to a higher frequency of light. You will still engage with the world through a distinct personality structure, except this will now be harmonized with your soul.

This is the goal of creative evolution as you transition towards the New Earth.

Chapter 64

Supramental Transformation

All right, so let's explore this further. In my incarnation as Mirra, Sri Aurobindo and I had been working on building a bridge between matter and spirit so that the supramental force could be anchored into the field of matter, accelerating and shaping the evolutionary journey of *Gaia*. How exactly does the weakening of magnetic fields, and the subsequent reversal, help with this transformation? Is it possible to consciously assist in this process, as many are now asking?

First of all, remember that the *saturnian matrix* is a grid structure anchored within the magnetic field of the Earth. As the magnetic field weakens so also does the power of this matrix. Imagine that this matrix is like a Pandora's Box. As the power of this matrix fades, all the contagions inside this box begin to spill out to the surface where they can be dissolved in the power of supramental light.

It is not necessary to take up arms against these contagions and shadows, simply to see them for what they are. As you become empty, and stay connected with higher levels of the mind, the power of the supramental will automatically dissolve the power of the old matrix, while preventing excessive breakdown and destruction. The new planetary grid is meanwhile getting stronger, allowing new patterns of human functioning to become stabilized.

As the timelines diverge, the rapidly growing nucleus of those who are preparing for supramental consciousness will become a point of resonance around which others can entrain, while those who choose to resist will leave their bodies with increasing rapidity.

The dark ones who are extensions of the anti-evolutionary forces will cling to their attempts to maintain power and dominion. They will struggle and create chaos for a while, but the supramental descent will rapidly seal their fate. As the frequency of matter increases, their base of power will disintegrate. The actors involved will self-implode. The Earth and the remainder of humanity will literally lift out of the denser bands where corruption has been allowed to exist.

What you call 'darkness' has had an important role to play in the awakening of greater 'light', It is time to honor all the actors in this divine drama now. Human beings are emotionally wired to learn from contrasts. Recognize that all events and experiences you are facing at this time are neither good nor bad but a process of discovering your yet unknown strength.

There is another aspect to this supramental force which is important to recognize. This force is capable of creating mutations within the biology of humans and other species. Sri Aurobindo would often speak about this, "A change of consciousness is the major fact of the next evolutionary transformation," he would often say. "Supramental consciousness, by its very nature, will impose any necessary mutations upon the body."

You tend to look at mutations as if they were something accidental, driven by a blind force of chance, a wild experiment where the outcome is likely to be bizarre and uncertain. And yet you see in the natural state a profoundly intricate and amazingly beautiful web of life where every species has its own unique and inter-dependent place. How is this possible if there isn't an underlying intelligence directing and shaping this process?

You also tend to look at mutations as if they need an external agent, some form of radiation perhaps, or else long eons of time, to break up existing models of DNA and initiate something new. But what if the driving force behind mutations isn't something external to nature, but a hidden force within nature itself, striving for diversity and self-perfection, which can very quickly create new forms of life when the conditions are right?

New species tend to emerge at the end of magnetic reversals as existing species die off and *Gaia* chooses to repopulate herself through the action of incoming cosmic and gamma rays. There is an intelligence within nature which is capable of orchestrating this feat. How much more is possible when a race of conscious human is able to participate in this process?

What Sri Aurobindo makes clear is that humans have the capacity to holographically link with the hidden powers of nature, and help turn on the genetic codes necessary to access and shape this evolutionary transformation. It does not require many people, only that these people are empty enough so that the power of the *Mother* can move through them. These few weigh more than the many.

Your experiments with artificial intelligence and attempts to forge some form of alliance with a world of robots and machines falls far short of *Gaia's* capacity for conscious evolution. These experiments arise from the rational level of the mind, and are therefore limited in conception and scope. But imagine what is possible when you learn to access the higher levels of the mind, ultimately even the supramental level, in order to merge with the consciousness of *Gaia*, and consciously participate in the goal of new creation!

The supramental journey is about creating a pathway in consciousness. You move your awareness out to merge with *Gaia* and with the Cosmos, and then bring higher fields of creative consciousness down through your bodies into the heart of matter. Supramental consciousness has the power to transform reality, and shape evolution, in a way that your rational consciousness cannot. This is the secret of alchemy and self-transcendence.

It requires enormous dedication and effort, but is the path that nature has now chosen.

Know that each challenge is also an opportunity. You carry within yourselves everything you need to make your realization complete. Where there are thick shadows, there is also somewhere a great light, and where this light descends, deep shadows will come to the surface.

There will be wars and rumors of wars, there will be hunger and death, there will be great suffering as shadows of greed, oppression and colonialism are released. Remember that a *supramental descent* is always accompanied by a *supramental catastrophe*, and that the harmonizing power of truth-consciousness will ultimately transform the subconscious shadows of history.

As supramental light descends to earth, and the soul incarnates fully, a new evolution becomes possible, not merely on a personal level but within the collective. As you mature into your divinity, you understand that this path of planetary service becomes the only path worth travelling.

Chapter 65

The Inconscient

The creation of each species is the result of new involutionary energy descending from the archetypal realm known as the Overmind. In this case, however, the new human species will be birthed from involutionary energies emerging directly from the Supermind, a hidden force of divine intent arising within the Deep Inconscient.

As waves of supramental awareness enter physical creation from beyond the veils of time and space, it awakens the power of the dragons asleep within the realms of unconscious matter. A wild profusion of creative energy follows. The spell of matter is broken. You arise from the sleep of a thousand years into the fulness of your creative powers. You become the voice of *Gaia* calling new species into existence.

Until you achieve a unified awareness where you are fully joined with the heart and soul of *Gaia*, it is not necessary to impose human concepts onto the powerful tides of evolution. Since you innately have a resonance to various orders of life, an alignment with distinct star systems, an affinity with different species on Earth, it is enough to simply be a channel, and allow a greater intelligence to move through.

You are invited, however, to voice your highest intents, prayers and visions, which become a blueprint for the New Earth. Every species that has ever lived continues its existence within the morphogenetic fields of *Gaia*. It has also been shown that DNA can be transmitted across galaxies through memory fields held within photons of light. Once *Gaia* awakens to the Supermind, she can use all the potential imprinted within these cosmic seed banks to shape new orders of evolution.

Any resistance to the supramental descent will crumble during the magnetic reversal. With the release of DMT, enormous doorways will be opened between dimensions. New genetic information will flow through these doorways in the form of intricate patterns of sacred geometry, similar to geometries often seen in ayahuasca visions.

These geometries will shape the codes of life so that new species can emerge at the request of *Gaia*, supported and assisted by the elemental kingdoms. This new information can then go out across the universe through these same resonant fields.

All new species emerge from the *Inconscient* in response to an involutionary wave. I have used this term earlier, but never bothered to define it properly. The *Inconscient* is the Dark Womb of Creation, the hiding place of the Self within Matter. The same Inconscient that creates a veil of Ignorance within your physical universe is also the birthing place for all new evolution.

Your senses normally operate within a very narrow band of sensory input. If this input was suddenly enhanced, your human mind and nervous system would be incapable of handling these new layers of reality. In the same way, the Inconscient serves as a reality-constricting valve for involutionary energy, in the absence of which there would be a profusion of creative input too overwhelming to sustain in third-dimensional reality.

Evolution is a gradual process of raising Self-Awareness within the realm of matter, until such a time that matter becomes plastic enough to experience the full impact of the Self reflected within itself.

With the entry of the Supramental Force into the heart of the Inconscient, and into the mind of the cells, evolution can now make a quantum leap. There is a potential now for Creator-consciousness to become Self-aware within Creation, triggering an enormous flowering of evolutionary capacities within all species of life. The divine *Shakti*, asleep within the heart of Creation, starts to awaken. Physical matter itself becomes more *plastic* to sustain the full impact of Her divine force and power.

At this stage you find that your body becomes directly responsive to the power of your intention. Aging, disease and death fall away. You have become empty enough that the vast ocean of primordial consciousness can flow through. You are ready now to enter the evolutionary stream of the seventh root race, *homo universalis*.

Chapter 66

Seventh Universe

When indigenous people such as the Inkas spoke of *Pachamama*, they were referring to *Mother Earth*. But they were also referring to the Sun, Moon, Stars, Galaxies, and to the physical Universe itself. They were addressing the *Great Mother* that exists at the heart of all Creation, and which cannot be divided.

It is time for us to now enter into a new understanding of *Gaia*, based on this awareness of non-duality. From the perspective of our senses there is division and multiplicity in the world. From the perspective of the rational mind, this translates as an experience of duality. But when we enter the perspective of the intuitive mind, this apparent division drops away. And when we enter the realm of *Gaia* as soul, we recognize in her the same *Great Mother* that moves through all aspects of Creation, including ourselves.

Our relationship with the *Great Mother* is changing. As supramental light enters deeper into the realms of the Inconscient, the creativity and power of the *Great Mother* can no longer be restrained. In relating to *Gaia* as the *Great Mother*, we also free within ourselves an infinite power of creativity and love.

Sri Aurobindo glimpsed that the current universal cycle is different from the six universal cycles that have preceded it. In the history of the universe there have been six consecutive periods which began with a creation, were sustained by a force of preservation, and ended with destruction. But he saw that the seventh cycle would be different. It would be a progressive manifestation which would express the Divine more and more completely, so that no disintegration would be necessary.

This has been my own experience as well. It began with the descent of the Supermind into the heart of the Inconscient. This has not happened before. Your collective subconscious still holds memories of prior cataclysms and destruction, and you therefore expect that any process of transformation must be accompanied by doom and gloom. But this is no longer necessary. With the supramental force now starting to penetrate the Inconscient, you are quickly entering an age of plasticity where physical substance, including the physical body, is no longer subject to the laws of entropy and death.

This also applies to recurring cosmic events such as galactic superwaves, solar micronova and geomagnetic reversals. The application of the supramental force to these phenomena, means that rather than going through cycles of extinction and new creation, new timelines based on progressive manifestation can now be initiated.

It may be that many humans are still too identified with the forces of dissolution, and not plastic enough to make this Shift with their physical bodies intact. On a planetary level, however, *Gaia* has been able to enter deep into the Inconscient. I haven't spoken of Aisha in a while, but this has been her own task, and she has accomplished what was necessary. *Gaia* is prepared to ride the supramental wave, and need not recapitulate earlier cycles of catastrophe and extinction. Instead, she can use the cosmic electricity entering from solar and galactic forces to shape realties not yet imagined!

All new species in the past have emerged from an involutionary intent descending from the archetypal realm of the *overmind*. With the Inconscient now opening to the light of Truth-Consciousness from beyond the veils of Creation, a new level of mind is emerging to guide the evolutionary process. The next species of humanity will emerge from the action of the *supermind*.

As supramental consciousness permeates the depths of the Inconscient, this hiding place for the Self can no longer remain hidden. The supermind represents the fullness of the Self within a matrix that is immeasurably more plastic, where physical matter is transformed into a vibrational frequency known as 'true matter'. Even the seemingly immutable laws of physics and nature are undergoing change in response to this emergence.

The Seventh Universe was initiated with the supramental descent in 1956. As supramental consciousness enters the Inconscient to awaken the sleeping power of the dragons, you are collectively entering a progressive cycle of evolution much more rapidly than what was possible before, and no longer need to fall back into unconsciousness. As you experience the plasticity of *true matter*, every last vestige of a dualistic worldview will soon disintegrate.

Over the next few centuries, humanity will evolve into its perfection. And simultaneously, a new planetary entity, *Gaia Luminous*, will emerge from the Womb of Creation.

Chapter 67

Gaia Luminous

All right, I am going to take off my teacher hat now. This role can be important when I wish to share ideas and perspectives, but it also gets a bit tedious, since I can get a bit too identified with it sometimes. I prefer to be a storyteller instead, or simply a guide.

What with jumping around in time, and focusing on events yet to come, I haven't said much about Aisha or my family lately. Perhaps you are also wondering what's been going on with me as Elmira, for I haven't said much about this incarnation since that underworld journey in Shambala.

I mentioned already that Shambala exists within the causal body of the Earth. If I say that it is located in the core of the Earth it would be tempting for you to think in terms of distance, and imagine this as a third dimensional space, but the properties of the causal planes are different. It is actually more a space than a place.

In Shambala you have direct access to your causal body. This means you can directly touch the causal body of the Earth, which is in essence the heart of *Gaia*. This is why so many masters and adepts like to visit there, or even make this their home.

Some of you may have had an experience of the causal planes in your dreams, or in between lifetimes after you drop your physical body, and eventually even the astral body. It is the natural home of the soul, where you experience your multi-dimensionality most easily. Being in Shambala offers you the experience of being multi-dimensional while still retaining your physical body.

For many of the Guardians, and for Aisha herself, this is where they found themselves able to influence planetary evolution in the most effective way possible. Being in Shambala, she could work directly with the meridians and leylines of the Earth, and join her own consciousness with the soul consciousness of *Gaia*.

This means she could enter the soul of the Earth, and become part of this herself. You will need to drop the concept of size and distance if you wish to understand what this means, but essentially this implies that in joining the soul of the Earth she also *became* the soul of the Earth, and that her own state of expanded awareness could now permeate all the way through the astral, etheric, and eventually the physical body of the Earth.

My own attempts to achieve the supramental descent thus allowed her to anchor this field through all the dimensions of *Gaia*. With the support of the dragons, elemental beings, nature spirits, and guardians who work tirelessly for the evolution of consciousness, this supramental force is now permeating through the leylines and energy matrix of the Earth.

There will come a time when the *saturnian matrix* completely dissolves and the *organic matrix* is fully established. I have outlined the mechanics of this, but know that there are many beings working behind the scenes to ensure that this will happen. This work will continue until your entire planet is established within the supramental realms.

I have spoken often about future root races emerging for humanity, *homo luminous* and *homo universalis*. Aisha's task has been similar, except on a planetary level. It is her job to support the emergence of a supramentalized planet, *Gaia Luminous,* a fourth density world capable of developing the evolutionary codes necessary to extend this morphogenetic field across all dimensions to birth the seventh universe.

Chapter 68

Himalayan Outpost

And what about Issa and Mirjan? They continued their work for a while with the ashram they had founded next to the Dal Lake in Srinagar. Later, needing more solitude, they retreated, along with their disciples, deeper into the Himalayas. Most of these disciples had also eventually taken the rainbow body, and so it was not uncommon from time to time for the entire company to move their base to a new location.

Their task was to continue inspiring specific individuals whom they felt had the potential to blaze a light within the darkness. This included scientists, philosophers, alchemists, inventors and spiritual teachers. Some of them became known as ascended masters, showing up where needed at pivotal times in earth's history, while others remained working for humanity behind the scenes. Some of them would take brief incarnations from time to time to initiate a specific mission, just as I did with Mirra Alfassa, before continuing their work in immortal bodies.

These adepts number in their thousands today, and continue seeking for those who are ready to serve *Gaia* and the new humanity. I imagine that some of you reading this book will find yourselves being inspired to join this great work. Call on these adepts with clear intention, and they will find you.

There are stories circulating about some of these adepts and masters in your spiritual literature. Their stories have inspired many, and includes those whose names may be familiar to some of you. Although I will not infringe on their anonymity, if you manage to piece together some hints I have given, you may even be able to identify some of them, including my own parents!

Meanwhile, Hiranya and Arwyn had become ambassadors between the nature kingdoms, the *fae* people, and the *inner earth tribes*. The *fae* do not need to create a rainbow body since they have access to an elixir of immortality, which allows them to travel through dimensions and maintain their bodies as long as they wish. They would often meet with Aisha in Shambala, helping to set the stage for a time when the *inner earth tribes,* the *fae* people, and the *star nations,* will be ready to establish contact with surface humans again.

The task of Eliyakim and Sara has been more specific. They remain within the incarnational cycles, and have been helping to create an archetype for the balance of masculine and feminine energies in human relationship. This is an arena where humans seem to need help, for many human relationships suffer from hurts and expectations that get projected onto their partners, creating even more chaos.

As for myself, I notice I still haven't shared much about myself since those days in Shambala. I feel a strange reluctance to do so, for I have always shied away from calling too much attention to myself. As an embodiment of *Shakti,* I find myself being much more connected with a planetary or universal identity, rather than with a personal self, and so my human story feels somewhat unimportant in this larger context.

But I will say that I have been spending time in close partnership with Aisha in Shambala, although not as much time as I would like, since much of my work also has been about understanding and joining with human consciousness in order to refine and create new genetic pathways. I do occasionally overlight those among the surface humans who invite me to do so, such as the one who has chosen now to write this story.

Unlike my parents and my brothers, I have not had the fortune of sharing my life with a partner. Perhaps this is because I have come to this Earth from beyond the known dimensions, beyond the polarity of what is commonly experienced here as masculine and feminine. Perhaps it is because the task of creating a new root race requires that I hold an uninterrupted and integrated balance of both these elements within my own being. Or perhaps it is not time yet, and I simply await one who is able to meet me in this space within the supramental worlds.

Chapter 69

The Supramental World

"Awake, O sleeper in the ignorant night,
A new sun is born into the human sky;
Even in the darkness of the unconscious world,
The divine light is born in secret hearts."

– Sri Aurobindo, Savitri

My intention for releasing this manuscript has been to hold out a candle in the midst of the ignorance and darkness of these times. As your world descends into human catastrophe and chaos, can you keep your eyes on a larger hope, trusting that there is more to existence than what you see and hear with your outer senses, that a supramental world awaits past the Orwellian realities you currently face?

If you are here on earth at this time, and if you have been drawn to this manuscript, it is because you are part of a new story. As you cross the threshold of a supramental world, and initiate the birthing of a new species, I am here to walk with you. My role is not that of a distant observer but an active participant in this grand transformation—a gatekeeper, guide and guardian of this cosmic vision.

As you enter this new world, the wars and divisions that have long plagued humanity will fade into insignificance. The truth of your interconnectedness will become self-evident. As personal ego dissolves in the wall of flames guarding this realm, you will discover in its place the forces of empathy, love and beauty inviting you to join the heartbeat of the universe.

In the absence of the *saturnian grid*, your latent abilities will flower, and a new spiritual landscape be revealed to your senses. Your body will become an expression of divine intention, as matter itself becomes supple and plastic. New possibilities of existence will be revealed as the natural world comes into resonance with the emergence of a divine human species.

Inner earth realms have been awaiting the moment when surface humanity is ready to acknowledge its divinity, and will gladly join your evolutionary stream as you make this Shift. As the *fae* kingdoms and galactic humans make contact, you will find yourself having access to technologies and abilities long forgotten, based on a fluidity of life and purpose.

What else can I tell you? You will find that transformation is not a solitary journey but a collective dance. Co-operation will replace competition, unity will overcome discord, and a shared sense of purpose will bind minds and hearts together. As the veils of *maya* dissolve, you will find a quality of grace and power permeating all things.

The transition into the Supramental world is not just a change of scenery but a profound metamorphosis of the human spirit. It is a journey that transcends the boundaries of the known and opens the door to uncharted territories of consciousness. As you pass through the veils of *maya* and realize your essential divinity, the *kanchukas* will fall away.

In *Daughter of the Moon*, Aisha shares with Mirjan about how the *kanchukas* were created. As Primordial Consciousness first began to permeate into the Inconscient, nature was not yet prepared to express the fulness of this Presence. The knowledge of Eternity was lost, as you began to shrink your identity to a single incarnation in space and time. The knowledge of Infinity was lost, as you turned from the knowledge of fullness to a belief in limitation, resulting in a constant craving for something you felt was missing.

Likewise the knowledge of Omnipresence, Omniscience and Omnipotence became condensed into limited presence, limited knowledge and limited abilities. What happens when you begin to journey back through these veils and discover your unlimited power and presence as Divine Creators?

This transition into the supramental world is an invitation to explore the depths of your own consciousness, and to walk the path of conscious evolution, leading to a reality beyond anything you have currently known or understood, a reality where the collective human spirit is reborn in unity and wisdom. It involves the creation of new genetic pathways, and the birth of a new human species.

The emergence of *homo luminous* is no longer a distant dream. This blueprint has been established within the subtle dimensions of the Earth, and will soon become externalized in a world of *true matter*. Look to the eastern horizon, for a new dawn is at hand.

Children of the Stars

As I come to the end of my story, yours is just beginning. My role has been to shape the emergence of a new species. As a child of the stars, I remember my galactic origins, and who I AM beyond the veil. You too are now discovering yourself as children of the stars, remembering who you are in all dimensions of space, time and beyond.

When you first met me in *Daughter of the Moon*, I was a six-year-old child who had just been told she would become the *manu* for the *sixth root race,* the sun-eyed children who would emerge on this Earth. How well I remember when Aisha asked me if I was willing to choose this, and the rapturous excitement I felt upon hearing these words.

As I look back on my life from the perspective of those of you reading these words, I feel immensely grateful for being given this role, and for all the support I have received from so many beings in fulfilling this. I suppose it is not very different from being an actor on a stage, playing a role that can inspire people, and doing the best you can, knowing that ultimately there is a greater stage than anything outside you, a greater script than anything that could be written, and a supreme director who chooses each actor in this great play of life.

I remember well Sri Aurobindo at the end of his life, continuing for the hundredth time to perfect his epic masterpiece, *Savitri,* even when his eyes had become too dim to see clearly. He recognized that this was not just a poem but rather an act of creation. The words that were written brought to life something in the collective field of possibility that had only been latent before.

I too am a dreamer of worlds. It does not matter so much if anyone ever reads this manuscript, although I have asked the *Mother* to take this message out wherever it needs to go. Dreaming my life has been enough to create a new timeline, a *sunlit path* that will find those who are ready to walk that way. For this is the role I was given by the *Mother*, along with the incarnation of Shiva known as Sri Aurobindo. We were to establish a genetic pathway for the *sun-eyed children of a new dawn.*

These pathways are governed, not by subconscious limitations carried over from the past, but by the vast uncharted territory of human potential. Those of you reading this manuscript, and feeling yourselves somehow touched and inspired, please know that just like these words, my presence remains with you as well.

I would like to end this manuscript then with one of my favorite passages from *Savitri*:

> *I saw them cross the twilight of an age*
>
> *The sun-eyed children of a marvelous dawn*
>
> *Great creators with wide brows of calm*
>
> *The massive barrier-breakers of the world*
>
> *Laborers in the quarries of the gods...*
>
> *The architects of immortality*
>
> *Into the fallen human sphere they came*
>
> *Faces that wore the Immortal's glory still...*
>
> *Bodies made beautiful by the spirit's light...*
>
> *Carrying the Dionysian cup of joy*

Lips chanting an unknown anthem of the soul
Feet echoing in the corridors of Time
High priests of wisdom, sweetness, might and bliss
Discoverers of beauty's sunlit ways...
Their tread one day shall change the suffering earth
And justify the light on Nature's face.

Epilogue

The story of my life has been written. I am Elmira, who came from the stars and fell to this earth in response to a call. I found myself expressing this story through one who was open to receiving me, who sits on the keyboard now, who continues to dance with me through further chapters of life even after this story has been written.

It is true that the dreamer is never separate from the dream. Was it I, Elmira, who dreamed Kiara Windrider into existence, chasing him down through the wide river of time, so he could find me inside himself? Did he dream me up? Are we both part of an archetypal story bigger than either of us, yearning to find expression in a single shared heart? Who is the dreamer and what is the dream?

Kiara sits at his keyboard now dreaming new worlds into existence, worlds that span a multitude of incarnations and infinite timelines of existence. He understands this journey, and it is what he has always lived for, why he came to earth many decades ago in earth time. He was called by the Great Mother, and learned to give himself to her, to see her in all things, to love her in all forms, to shape her evolutionary journey on earth.

In his childhood years he felt often lonely, for this dream had been carrying him long before he understood its message. A stranger in a strange land, he wondered sometimes if he had dropped down on the wrong planet, or if he would ever find his tribe.

In later years he did find his tribe, but even so most of them were not in human form. Like me, he learned to listen to the wind as it touched his skin, the whispers of silence that spoke through a mountain lake, the powerful emotions that pulsed through thunderous ocean surf. He came to glimpse the seasons of time and the cycles of galactic history that vibrated within his soul.

As he learned to listen, there came others of his tribe from beyond the material veil who began to communicate with him and through him. He wondered often if he was simply making up stories to escape from the harshness of a fractured collective. Eventually, however, he learned to trust the sources who spoke through him, and the guidance he was being given.

And so it was that this story found him, my parents Issa and Mirjan, my brothers Hiranya and Eliyakim, my teacher Aisha, and the guardians of Shambala. As we shared our stories through his receptive consciousness, I felt my longings became his own, my vibrational frequency moved through his body as well, and my dreams became real inside him.

The task of becoming a *manu* cannot be done in isolation, at least not for the root races to come. It requires a great sensitivity to emerging morphogenetic fields, a balance that harmonizes masculine and feminine, spirit and matter, heaven and earth. My longing for embodiment initiates a new dream upon this earth, sparked into resonance by those who are now reading this manuscript, those who recognize themselves as part of this shared purpose.

As the characters within this dream begin to find each other, I continue to incarnate myself within the density of matter as *manu* of the sixth root race. Of this unfolding journey, many more books could be written, but it is part of your human story now, and will be unveiled when the time is right.

Glossary

Ahamkara – sense of personal self that emerges from the thoughts, feelings and memories of a given incarnation

alchemy – a transformational process

asmita siddha – the mind of light, attuned to higher realms of consciousness

Atma, jiva or *jivatma* – individuated spark of divinity

avatar – direct descent of light with all its attributes

brahman, paramatma – universal soul, or ultimate reality

bodhisattva – one who comes to earth to help humanity, usually in the lineage of the Buddha

buddhi – centers related to wisdom and intuition within the *vignanamayakosha*

buddha – illumined one, title given to Prince Siddhartha after he achieved enlightenment

chakras – energy centers

devas – elementals, angels, fairies, or extra-terrestrial beings *dharma* – path of soul destiny

fae, elves, or *sidhe* – races of humans, such as the Tuatha de Danann, existing in dimensions invisible to most mortals

fairies – elemental beings, such as gnomes, dwarves, sylphs, pixies, and garden spirits, whose work is to help support physical life on *Gaia*

guardians – elder beings working behind the scenes for planetary evolution

Indra's net – a metaphor from *mahayana buddhism* referring to how all things are holograhically related to each other

Inner Earth – regions below the surface of the earth populated by various civilizations and entities in physical, etheric, astral and causal dimensions of existence

kanchukas – subconscious self-limiting veils – there are 5 kanchukas within the veil of *maya*

karma – action, the law of karma is a reminder that there are consequences to every action

kaya siddha – enlightenment of the physical body, activation of the cellular mind to awareness of unity in all things

koshas – vehicles for the soul. There are five interpenetrating koshas, ranging from the physical body (*annamayakosha*) to energy body (*pranamayakosha*) to mind body (*manomayakosha*) to wisdom body (*vignanamayakosha*) to soul body (*anandamayakosha*)

kundalini – life force energies emanating from the union of subtle, astral and causal bodies, flowing across channels known as *nadis*, and often associated with the experience of *enlightenment*

lokas – worlds and dimensions

maa, mataji – beloved mother

manas – centers related to rational mind and emotion held within the *manomaykosha*

Manu – founder of a root race, one who carries the blueprint of this race within their consciousness

maya – can be perceived as a veil of illusion but also as the goddess of creation

metteya, maitreya, messiah, masih – gatherer, deliverer, liberator that was expected to come in Buddhist and Hebrew traditions

nath or *nath yogis* – lineage of immortals in Himalayan tradition, going back to Gorakh Nath and to Shiva himself.

nirmana kaya – body of light, immortal body, rainbow body

Paramatma or *Brahman* – universal consciousness

prakriti – objective reality

pralaya – catastrophic phenomena related to the turning of an Age

psychic center – another term for the evolving soul

purusha – subjective reality

Self – the primordial consciousness at the heart of all things

shining ones, also known as *devas* – an angelic or extra-terrestrial race

Shakti – primordial energy, counterpart of shiva

Shambhala – an etheric city existing close to the center of the Earth, part of a network of etheric, astral and causal worlds collectively known as *Agartha*

Shiva – primordial consciousness. alternatively, one of the three forces representing creation, of which Brahma is creator, Vishnu is preserver and Shiva is destroyer

soul – center of identity within the causal planes, reflection of the *atma*, or primordial Self, within terrestrial evolution

spanda – primordial sound, sound of creation pervading all things *tantra* – path of raising the kundalini from root to crown, in order to unite shiva with shakti

tattwas – building blocks of the universe, literally means 'the thats'

Tuatha de Danann – a race of higher dimensional humans, or *elves*, residing in Ireland

Tukhara or *Tocharian* – settlers in Kashmir who originated in the central steppes of Asia, part of the lineage of Issa

tulku – recognized reincarnation of a high lama (Buddhist tradition)

vimana – vehicle of light

yugas – cosmic cycles or world ages. There are four *yugas* in each cosmic cycle, known as *satya yuga, treta yuga, dwapara yuga* and *kali yuga*. They move in a descending cycle from light to darkness, and then in an ascending cycle from darkness to light. We are currently in an ascending cycle at the crossing point between *kali yuga* and *dwapara yuga*. They can be understood in terms of our Sun's orbit around its twin star, sometimes understood as Sirius, in their shared journey around the Galactic Center.

About Kiara Windrider

Kiara Windrider spent much of his early life traveling and practicing various spiritual traditions in India. A lifelong interest in environmental awareness, peacemaking, and social justice led to a dual degree in Peace studies and International Development through Bethel College, North Newton, Kansas.

Later, he completed a graduate program in Transpersonal Counseling Psychology through JFK University in Orinda, California, and worked for many years at an alternative psychiatric center called Pocket Ranch Institute, which specialized in healing emotional trauma and facilitating spiritual emergence. He received a psychotherapy license (MFT) from the State of California in 1998. He has also trained in various forms of bodywork, breathwork, hypnotherapy, and shamanic healing.

Kiara is an avid science researcher, exploring connections between galactic cycles, climate change, ancient history, quantum physics, human behavior and spiritual awakening. As an outcome of this extensive research he has come to the firm conviction that we stand collectively at the brink of a quantum evolutionary leap beyond our wildest dreams.

He is currently focused on planetary healing using a system of anchoring divine light known as Ilahinoor. He also teaches Inka shamanic practices, into which he was initiated by Juan Nunez del Prado and Ivan Nunez del Prado. Kiara has worked with Egyptian, Huna and Sufi traditions, and is also rooted in Integral Yoga, Kashmir Shaivism, and the Advaita traditions of India.

He offers workshops and retreats worldwide for awakening to our infinite potential. His greatest wish is to live fully in the wonder of each moment, and to help awaken this beautiful planet to its luminous destiny.

Kiara is the author of *Doorway to Eternity: A Guide to Planetary Ascension, Year Zero: Time of the Great Shift, Ilahinoor: Awakening the Divine Human, Gaia Luminous: Emergence of the New Earth, Homo Luminous: Manual for the Divine Human, Issa: Son of the Sun, Mirjan: Daughter of the Moon,* and *Elmira: Child of the Stars.*

Please check out his website, Kiarawindrider.net, as well as his Facebook and YouTube channels. Suggestions and comments are always welcome, and may be addressed to kiara@eternaldoorway.com.